GUITAR *signature licks*

BEST OF
WES MONTGOMERY

by Wolf Marshall

Front cover photo by Tom Copi / Frank Driggs Collection
Back cover photo by Joe Alper / Frank Driggs Collection

ISBN 978-0-634-00902-0

HAL•LEONARD®
CORPORATION
7777 W. BLUEMOUND RD. P.O. BOX 13819 MILWAUKEE, WI 53213

Visit Hal Leonard Online at
www.halleonard.com

CONTENTS

FOREWORD

This is the first Signature Licks transcription book/CD to explore the guitar style of Wes Montgomery. It is designed as both a stylistic profile and a resource for enlarging your musical palette. It can be approached in several ways. For the neophyte, it will serve as a wonderful introduction to the art of jazz guitar. The tablature format will invite even the non-reader to experience this rich and fascinating music. Remember: Montgomery himself was not a reader. For the intermediate player, it is a valuable source book and a means for developing the ear, learning the jazz guitar lexicon, and developing greater improvisation skills. Rock, pop, and blues guitarists alike will find countless intriguing licks here to add to their arsenals. Advanced guitarists, particularly those accomplished in other styles, will benefit tremendously from the note-for-note transcriptions, technical analysis of Montgomery's improvisations, and accompanying audio tracks. For those musicians, a recommended goal would be to physically master and memorize a piece, and to recreate its actual performance at tempo with the accompanying recording. The benefits of spending time like this in "the woodshed" will be enormous and immediately apparent. Accordingly, this volume deviates from my previous works in that there is a greater emphasis on performance with longer play-along tracks as befits the jazz repertory. Sheer physical space would not allow a blow-by-blow description of every musical event—especially in the multi-chorus environment of jazz improvisation. Suffice it to say Wes Montgomery's music teems with signature licks. To cite each one and play it slowly would be impractical, and beyond the scope of this volume. As a happy consequence, each musical selection can be presented in its full glory. Enjoy.

—Wolf Marshall

INTRODUCTION

Wes Montgomery was the guiding force behind the second great epoch of modern jazz guitar. If we consider the first as having started with the early experiments of Charlie Christian in the late 1930s and early 1940s, then the next revolution belongs to Wes Montgomery. Like the musical cataclysm caused by Christian's solo flights, Montgomery had a resoundingly powerful impact on his contemporaries. Virtually all established guitarists went scurrying back to the woodshed—to re-evaluate their own approaches, to incorporate his patented octave playing and "impossible" block chording into their music, or to emulate his warm, fleshy tone, blues-based conception, and strongly swinging rhythmic feel. Jazz guitar music itself has come to be defined by his presence as either pre-Montgomery or post-Montgomery in concept and level of performance, and practically every jazz guitarist to emerge after his appearance has borne the mark of his influence—Joe Pass, George Benson, Pat Martino, Pat Metheny, Emily Remler, Larry Carlton, and Lee Ritenour, to name a handful.

Wes Montgomery's influence was all-encompassing—affecting, directly or indirectly, the studio scene and film scores, easy listening and pop records, R&B, the incipient genre of rock (heard variously in the music of Santana, Jimi Hendrix, the Grateful Dead, the Doors, and many others), and even country guitar. His contribution is at the core of universal guitar music, crossing over the borders that separate diverse players stylistically. It is alluded to in the work of the heaviest rock guitarists (Steve Vai, Paul Gilbert, et al.), and is quoted outright in the repertory of players like Stevie Ray Vaughan and Eric Johnson while being equally at home in TV commercials, all forms of contemporary popular music, and the syrupy "Muzak" (elevator music) format.

A THUMBNAIL HISTORY

By the time Wes Montgomery emerged from the fairly obscure club scene of his native Indianapolis in 1959, he was already something of a legend to the jazz intelligentsia and an appreciative circle of his peers. The normally reserved composer/musician/historian Gunther Schuller threw aside any detached and clinical observations and proclaimed his ability as: "Extraordinarily spectacular…unbearably exciting," and his musicality as possessing "purity of ideas" and "unfailing dramatic effectiveness." Renowned saxophonist Cannonball Adderley, who had seen and heard it all, practically broke down the doors at Riverside Records to deliver his personal recommendation: "There's this guitarist from Indianapolis! You've got to get him for the label! Here's his phone number!" And poll-winning jazz guitarist Jim Hall affectionately related the tongue-in-cheek story of spending the better part of a week fruitlessly "trying to catch Montgomery's thumb in a car door." That famous "Montgomery thumb" to which Hall was referring was part and parcel of the innovative and influential sounds we now readily recognize and cherish as the Wes Montgomery style.

To go back a bit…

Wes Montgomery was born John Leslie Montgomery in Indianapolis, Indiana, on March 6, 1923. He never received formal music training, but throughout his youth, he was interested in music and was encouraged by his older brother Monk (who later became famous for pioneering the Fender bass). In 1935, Monk bought him his first instrument, a $13 four-string tenor guitar on which Wes developed some basic technique. Wes Montgomery officially picked up the six-string guitar relatively late in life, at the age of 19. Initially inspired by the work of Charlie Christian (particularly the masterpiece "Solo Flight"), he taught himself by diligently copying Christian's solos from records. By the time he reached his twentieth birthday he was gigging regularly at the local 440 Club playing Charlie Christian solos.

Wes Montgomery's first professional break came when he secured a job with Lionel Hampton's band in 1948. Relentless touring and grueling road work made up his life for the next two years, and through the experience—he was exposed to musicians like Charlie Mingus, Fats Navarro, and Milt Bruckner—he became a seasoned jazz player. A devoted family man, Montgomery quit extensive touring in 1950 and stayed in Indianapolis afterward, playing sporadic club gigs mixed with non-musical day jobs. Montgomery's first recording session was with the Mastersounds (featuring his brothers Buddy and Monk on vibes and bass, respectively) on December 30, 1957, for Dick Bock's Pacific Jazz label. The tracks were released as the album *The Montgomery Brothers and Five Others*. Two other records were made by the Mastersounds: *Kismet* in 1958 and *The Montgomery/Land Quintet* in 1959. None of these releases brought Wes Montgomery widespread recognition.

Wes Montgomery recorded his first album as a leader for Riverside Records, thanks largely to the enthusiastic recommendation of Cannonball Adderley. Sessions took place on October 5th and 6th, 1959, at Reeves Sound Studios in New York. The record, *The Wes Montgomery Trio*, featured his regular working trio with Melvin Rhyne on organ and Paul Parker on drums. The organ trio (organ-guitar-drums) remained a favored setting for Montgomery throughout his career, and seemed to bring out his blues and funky jazz influences like no other ensemble. The material was a blend of medium tempo jazz standards, hard bop numbers, and Wes Montgomery originals. The reinterpreted classics "'Round Midnight" and "Yesterdays" remain outstanding and definitive Montgomery cuts to this day.

Things broke wide open for Wes Montgomery in 1960 with his next Riverside release, *The Incredible Jazz Guitar of Wes Montgomery*. Considered by many to be his finest jazz album, it featured luminaries Tommy Flanagan (piano), Percy Heath (bass), and Albert Heath (drums). Of the many excellent tracks on the record, Wes's originals "West Coast Blues" and "Four on Six" are stand-out tracks and have become bonafide jazz standards. As a result of the album, Montgomery began to receive long-overdue industry accolades and awards. That year he won the prestigious *Down Beat* Critic's New

Star award, a second place in the *Metronome* reader's poll, and was voted "Most Promising Jazz Instrumentalist" in *Billboard*.

The promise was fulfilled with the remaining Riverside albums, recorded from 1961 to 1964. Landmark albums to follow included *Boss Guitar, Full House, Movin' Along, So Much Guitar!*, and *Fusion!*. Wes Montgomery's last session for Riverside took place on November 27, 1963, and was heard on his Riverside record *Guitar on the Go*. And go it did: Wes Montgomery signed with Verve Records in 1964 and entered a new phase of his jazz career.

During the Verve years (1964–1966), and subsequently with A&M Records (1966–1968), Wes Montgomery produced records under the direction of Creed Taylor which gained larger commercial success with a pop audience—something of an anomaly in the jazz world. In this regard Montgomery was the first cross-over jazz artist, paving the way for the likes of George Benson, Chick Corea, Herbie Hancock, and the current smooth jazz genre. His efforts, though criticized by purists, were rewarded with a Grammy in 1967 for a slick version of "Goin' Out of My Head." Throughout these years, Montgomery also continued releasing straight-ahead jazz albums such as *Smokin' at the Half Note*, and his duo sessions with Jimmy Smith, as well as fine individual tracks like "Sun Down."

Wes Montgomery left us all too soon on June 15, 1968, the victim of a heart attack at the height of his popularity. Yet his legacy remains undiminished. He paved the way for new generations of jazz guitarists—evidenced in the work of George Benson, Pat Martino, Pat Metheny, Emily Remler, and virtually everyone else post-1959. Montgomery was the archetypal "fusion" musician, experimenting with varied ensemble settings from small bop combos to large orchestral groups with grandiose arrangements. His approach embraced every form of straight-ahead jazz and bebop as well as Afro-Cuban, Latin Rock, semi-classical, proto-funk, and pop styles. Wes Montgomery brought a freshness and vitality to jazz guitar that has not been surpassed or equaled. He is sorely missed.

DISCOGRAPHY

The titles in this volume came from the following records:

WES MONTGOMERY TRIO—Riverside 1156: "Missile Blues," "Yesterdays"
THE INCREDIBLE JAZZ GUITAR OF WES MONTGOMERY—Riverside 1169: "West Coast Blues"
FULL HOUSE—Riverside 9434: "Cariba," "I've Grown Accustomed to Her Face"
BOSS GUITAR—Riverside 9459: "Besame Mucho," "Fried Pies"
GUITAR ON THE GO—Riverside 9494: "Mi Cosa"
All the above-mentioned tracks are also available on the highly recommended 12-CD box set *WES MONTGOMERY: THE COMPLETE RIVERSIDE RECORDINGS*—Riverside 12RCD–4408–2

WES MONTGOMERY: THE SILVER COLLECTION—Verve 823 448–2: "Four on Six," "Misty"
CALIFORNIA DREAMING—Verve 827 842–2: "Sun Down"
ULTIMATE WES MONTGOMERY—Verve 314 539 787–2: "O.G.D." (aka "The Road Song")
The above-cited Verve tracks are also available on the excellent 2-CD compilation *WES MONTGOMERY: IMPRESSIONS—THE VERVE JAZZ SIDES*—Verve 521 690–2

Of inestimable value are the live Wes Montgomery performances contained on the following Vestapol videos: *LEGENDS OF JAZZ GUITAR VOLUME 1*—Vestapol 13009; *LEGENDS OF JAZZ GUITAR VOLUME 2*—Vestapol 13033; *WES MONTGOMERY 1965—BELGIUM*—Vestapol 13084.

THE RECORDING

Wolf Marshall: guitar
Mike Sandberg: drums and percussion
John Nau: piano and organ
Dennis Croy: bass

Recorded at Pacifica Studio and Marshall Arts Studio, Los Angeles, CA

Produced by Wolf Marshall

Special thanks to Brian Vance and Gibson USA for the outstanding guitar used on this recording. Wolf Marshall plays Gibson arch tops, Polytone and Fender amps, and Thomastik-Infeld flatwound Swing series strings.

Extra special thanks to Henry Johnson and Kenny Burrell for their help and insights into the Wes Montgomery style.

THE WES MONTGOMERY STYLE

TECHNIQUE

From the beginning, Wes Montgomery seemed to hear things differently on the instrument. Instead of pursuing the traditional plectrum style, he opted for a thicker, warmer tone produced by picking with the meat of his thumb. He created a uniquely personal sound in his single-note playing with this unorthodox, seemingly "impossible" physical approach. His tone and technique confounded and charmed the guitarists and audiences of his day. One glance at the currently re-issued video performances of Wes Montgomery (on Vestapol's *Legends of Jazz Guitar*) is more than telling, and continues to astonish us today.

Single notes

Wes Montgomery rested his plucking hand with fingers spread on the face of the guitar and the pickguard edge just behind the neck pickup. The thumb picked the strings with a relaxed stroke originating from the second joint. The thumb tip was cocked at the first joint in a backward angle, which has led many to believe that he was double-jointed. Montgomery used downstrokes predominately but could play long intricate lines with alternating strokes when desired.

Wes Montgomery's melodic conception has been described as horn-like—little wonder, as he drew great inspiration from musicians like Charlie Parker (alto sax), John Coltrane and Sonny Rollins (tenor sax), and Miles Davis (trumpet) in addition to conventional guitar sources such as Charlie Christian and Django Rheinhardt. The fingering of his single-note phrases, from simple melodious statements to earthy blues lines and florid bebop passages, has always been a source of consternation among jazz guitar purists. Like many blues and rock guitarists, Montgomery rarely used his pinky (fourth finger) for these phrases, irrespective of their complexity or physical demands. Furthermore, his technique was extremely linear. He frequently connected several positions laterally up and down the fretboard in one phrase, and often shifted on a single string. As a result, he seemed to avoid the normal positional confines of guitaristic "box playing." Instead, most of his lines overlapped and dovetailed each other in the manner of chord inversions arranged horizontally on the fingerboard.

Octaves

Wes Montgomery was an innovator and a pioneer. In his quest for sonic expansion, he developed a signature *parallel octave* approach which is arguably his most identifiable musical trait—particularly to the general public. An octave in this case is an interval eight steps apart, fingered as a dyad and articulated like a two-note chord. His facility with octaves remains unsurpassed to this day, as even a superficial listen to almost any Montgomery track will reveal. When playing octaves, he exploited two characteristic locked-fingering shapes:

Octaves

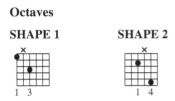

Shape 1 was for octaves played on the sixth and fourth strings, and on the fifth and third strings. Shape 2 was for octaves played on the fourth and second strings, and on the third and first strings. The deadened string, designated by X in the diagrams, is played by lightly but purposefully muting with the index finger of the fret hand. Montgomery also employed general muting with other left-hand fingers to deaden idle strings in a musical passage when playing octaves and chords.

The articulation for octaves was a variation of Montgomery's above-mentioned thumb attack. When playing octaves, he did not rest his fingers on the face of the guitar but lightly touched the pickguard and body. The stroke was a mixture of thumb and wrist motion, like a downstroke for strumming chords. Montgomery was famous for his improvised octave solos in tunes like "West Coast Blues," "Four on Six," "Besame Mucho" and "Fried Pies." He would also frequently play the entire head of a tune in octaves, as in "O.G.D. (The Road Song)" in this volume. The latter approach became a fixture of his later commercial style on Verve and A&M recordings.

Chords

One of the most compelling facets of Wes Montgomery's style was his chord playing. He had a natural gift for chord melody and was able to seamlessly integrate improvised block chording into his solo work—as in "Missile Blues," "Cariba," "Sundown," and countless others. His harmonic conception was "piano thinking" applied to guitar, and, at the time, seemed "impossible"—especially when considering the ease and smoothness with which he performed his chord passages, even at breakneck speeds. He just heard it that way, and again redefined the rules. Montgomery was equally adept at reharmonizing and rendering a melody (the head of a tune) with his block-chord approach, frequently adding uncommon and downright peculiar voicings to the harmonic framework. Cases in point are the striking performances heard in the standard "I've Grown Accustomed to Her Face" and his original composition "Mi Cosa." He played his chord phrases with a thumb-strumming attack, similar in articulation to his octave playing.

IMPROVISATION

Wes Montgomery was a master of melodic invention, having the facility, emotional content, taste, and originality to turn any piece into an engaging musical experience. As an improviser, Montgomery was concerned with *motivic development*, though in a natural and instinctive way. He was the consummate storyteller—leading an enthralled audience through chorus after chorus of inspired playing...revealing a motive here, developing it later, introducing a blues mood and then seasoning it with bebop modernism, chromatic tension, or pandiatonic superimposition. His motives and signature licks ran the gamut from simple blues ideas to complex bebop phrases. Like Coltrane and Parker,

Montgomery was always aware of where he was in the harmonic scheme, and he created his motivic activity accordingly. He constantly varied textures, rhythmic and harmonic complexity, and changes of register. Finally, regardless of the tempo, Wes Montgomery retained lyricism, fluidity, and clarity—and above all, *feel*—in all of his improvising.

IMPROVISING STRATEGY

Wes Montgomery created many of his best solos with great concern for form. Using the basic components of single notes, octaves, and block chords, he pursued a definite strategy: a general three-tier plan usually occurring over multiple choruses. Beginning with single-note playing in opening choruses, Montgomery progressed to octaves, and often reached a powerful climax of block chording in final choruses. This is dramatically presented in "West Coast Blues" in this volume. His climaxes were sometimes made more exciting with the use of a blues-based question-and-answer treatment of octave punches, interspersed with repeating chord figures reminiscent of a big band "shout chorus." This can be heard in the seventh and eighth choruses of "Missile Blues." The result of this structuring in improvised solos was a feeling of direction and cohesion, and of larger thematic development. Montgomery's sense of improvisation, guided by the order of form and balance of materials, was almost uncanny and precisely the sort of universal musicality which turned the jazz world on its collective ear, attracting even the non-jazz listener to his ingratiating guitar style.

EQUIPMENT

Wes Montgomery favored the sound and response of an arch-top, electric-acoustic guitar. He was closely identified throughout his career after 1960 with the Gibson L5 CES (Cutaway Electric Spanish) model, in varying configurations. L5s are single-cutaway (Florentine or Venetian), deep-bodied (3⅜") acoustics with F-holes and two built-in pickups. Judging by album jacket photos and publicity shots, Montgomery owned at least six different L5s from 1960 to 1968, two of which were custom-made single-pickup models. When playing the stock two-pickup style, he used the front (neck) pickup almost exclusively for its warmer tone; this is customary for the jazz guitar voice of the bebop genre. Prior to 1960, Montgomery used various other Gibsons. These included an L4 with a Charlie Christian bar pickup, an ES-125D and an ES-175. Kenny Burrell disclosed to me that Montgomery borrowed his L-7 and Fender Deluxe amp (not a Twin, as cited in previous accounts) for the 1959 recording session of *The Wes Montgomery Trio*. He was pictured on the cover of *The Incredible Jazz Guitar of Wes Montgomery* with an ES-175. Montgomery strung his guitars with Gibson HiFi flatwound strings, gauged from low to high: E=.058, A=.045, D=.035, G=.025 wound, B=.018, E=.014.

Wes Montgomery amplified his instruments during the Riverside years with either a late 1950s or early 1960s Fender tube amp. Reputedly, Rudy Van Gelder kept an old Fender Deluxe amp permanently on hand in his New Jersey studio where Wes recorded with Creed Taylor for Verve after 1963. Montgomery later switched to Standel Custom solid-state combo amps and alternated between these and Fender tube amps during the remainder of his career.

MISSILE BLUES
(The Wes Montgomery Trio)
By John L. (Wes) Montgomery

Figure 1—Head

"Missile Blues," an original composition, is a classic example of Wes Montgomery's transformation and enlargement of the blues idiom. The piece is in G and uses the 12-bar blues form, though the customary harmonic changes (I–IV–V) are avoided entirely in the head. Those changes are saved for the solo.

The main riff in measures 1–8 is a repeated two-bar figure made up of single notes and triads. The low G in the riff acts as a pedal point. Montgomery most likely fretted this with his left-hand thumb. His patented chain of diminished chords is played as a break in measures 9–10. This passage finds him harmonizing the eight-tone G diminished scale (whole-step/half-step: G–A–B♭–C–C♯–D♯–E–F♯) with diminished chords. This parallel motion with diminished chords occurs frequently in his style and is one of his most familiar traits. The turnaround is made of chromatically-descending, parallel 13th chords: B♭13–A13–A♭13–G7. Note the presence of the 9th in these chords as the highest note.

Figure 2—Solo and Head Out

In the blowing choruses, Montgomery plays over a modified 12-bar blues progression he favored, a progression sometimes referred to as "West Coast Changes." (See "West Coast Blues," also in this volume). This altered progression substitutes a series of ii–V changes (Cm7–F7, Bm7–E7, B♭m7–E♭7) for the standard IV7 and I7 chord in the sixth, seventh, and eighth measures of the form. Most of his improvised melodies conform to these alternate changes.

The nine-chorus solo A – I is a prime example of Montgomery's structured improvisational approach. The first three choruses are played in single notes, choruses 4 through 6 are played in octaves, and choruses 7 and 8 combine octaves and block chords. The final chorus is played entirely in block chords. Within that structure Montgomery makes a lot of inspired music.

The single-note choruses A B C are distinguished by a mixture of heady bop phrases and earthy blues licks. When playing diatonically on the I chord, Montgomery stays primarily in the G Mixolydian mode (G–A–B–C–D–E–F). On other changes he chooses either the corresponding scale, an arpeggio, or a melodic substitution. Arpeggio lines are pursued throughout. Noteworthy are the rhythmically displaced swing/blues riff (a paraphrase of Charlie Christian's "Air Mail Special" riff) in B measures 13–16, the string-of-eighths modulating bebop line in measures 19–24, and the quick triplet passage in C 25–26. The latter is an extended melody which emphasizes the higher intervals of bebop—the 9th, 11th, and 13th of the G7 chord—and is one of most technically challenging phrases in the solo. Other significant arpeggio lines include the B♭m7–E♭9 chord run in measure 8, the B♭ augmented triad (B♭–D–F♯) over C7 in measures 29–30, and the Am9 outline over D7 in measure 34. Montgomery plays a descending A♭ minor scale as a melodic substitute for G7 in measure 28—a classic bebop device which generates a ♯9–♭9–♯5–♭5 dissonance. A signature interval-leaping line is found in measures 32–33. This zigzagging contour contains the pattern of a leap followed by a step in the opposite direction to another leap again in the opposite direction, and so on. It is characteristic of Montgomery's handling of disjunct melodies.

Montgomery's octave solo is highly rhythmic and exciting. Each chorus is generally begun with a blues-oriented idea which gives way to extended arpeggio lines and bop melodies. Note the use of G minor pentatonic (G–B♭–C–D–F) in measures 37–41 and 48–50 to heighten the folkier blues effect. He adheres to this combined approach in the next two choruses F and G. Trademark lower-neighbor melodies are heard in measures 44, 47, and 59–60. An attractive melodic sequence is developed in measures 67–69. Note the varied rhythmic treatments of the three phrases in the sequence.

Montgomery begins to add block chords, largely as rhythmic punches, in G measures 73–79. At measure 80 he plays a signature block-chord passage of parallel diminished chords mixed with diatonic seventh chords. Note the strong melody line in the top voice of the chord phrase. Familiar blues licks are harmonized with parallel diminished chords and interspersed with octaves in measures 84–90. Notice the slurred augmented seventh chords in measure 88. From measure 90 to the end of the solo, Montgomery uses only block chords. Of particular interest are the numerous variations of his ii–V patterns in measures 92–94 and 102–106, the beautifully harmonized I–VI7–ii–V turnaround in measures 95–96, and the aggressive ninth chord episode in measures 97–100. The solo concludes with a return to one chorus of the head.

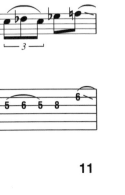

C 3rd Chorus

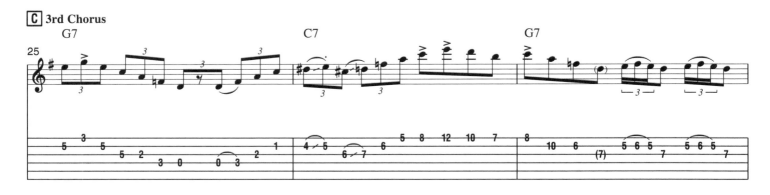

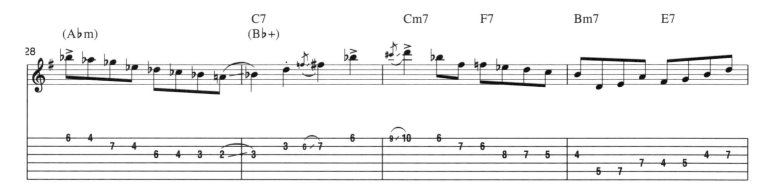

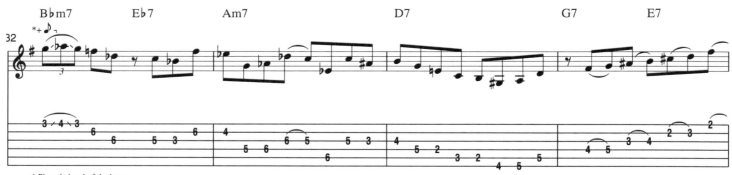

* Played ahead of the beat.

D 4th Chorus

* Mute inner string of octaves throughout.

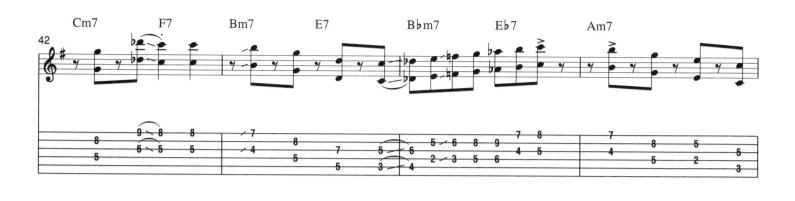

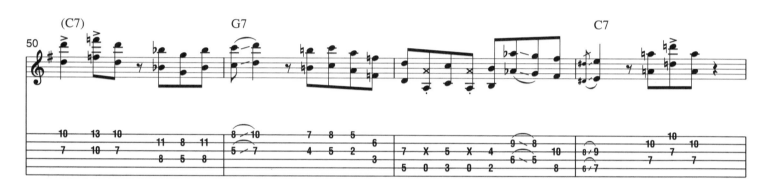

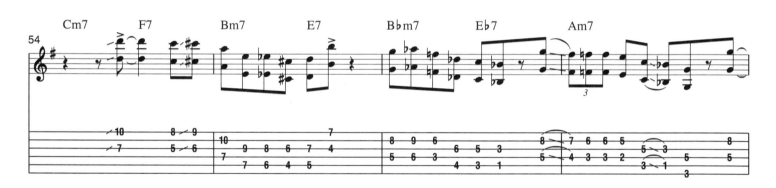

* organ plays A/G7

YESTERDAYS
from ROBERTA
(The Wes Montgomery Trio)
Words by Otto Harbach
Music by Jerome Kern

Figure 3—Head, Guitar Solo, and Outro

"Yesterdays" is a beautiful Jerome Kern standard in 32-bar ABAB (8–8–8–8) song form. The tune is in D minor with B sections that move through a cycle of fourths. Organist Melvin Rhyne did not solo on the track, leaving it wide open for a non-stop Montgomery showcase. As befits the tradition of the organ-trio genre, the group performed the tune as an easy-swinging minor blues with funk overtones.

The head is a sparse statement of the song's melody with blues-inflected embellishment. Much of it is situated in the first position and makes use of open strings. The D blues scale (D–F–G–A♭–A–C) decorates the melody in measures 1–4 and 17–20. A B♭m9 (B♭–D♭–F–A♭–C) arpeggio is used as a substitution over the A7♯5(♯9) chord in measure 16. The second time around (measures 31–32), an ostinato figure employing upper and lower neighbor notes to emphasize the A note acts as a pickup for the solo.

Montgomery's solo contains both blues and bop elements. It is comprised of single notes in the first 16 measures and concludes with octaves in the remainder of his improvisation. The single notes are played both in shorter, rhythmic phrases and in longer strings of eighth notes (as in measures 40–43 and 45–48). The solo begins with an angular intervallic melody arranged as a playful sequential phrase with a bouncy eighth/rest/eighth triplet rhythm. This is complemented by a phrase incorporating one of his favorite rhythmic motives, the syncopated five-note figure of quarter/eighth/quarter/eighth/quarter, in measures 37–39. In measures 40–41 he cultivates some uncommon sounds: a D7 arpeggio against E7, and E minor and B♭maj7♯5 over A7, before resuming more conventional bop lines in measures 42–44. The single-note portion closes with a climactic four-measure phrase. It is begun with a rising F Mixolydian (F–G–A–B♭–C–D–E♭) scale run in measures 45–46 over F13 and B♭9. Note the chromatic passing tones in the melody on beats 3 and 4 of measure 46. The melody turns around and descends via the D harmonic minor scale (D–E–F–G–A–B♭–C♯) in measures 47–48 to finish the section.

Montgomery's octave solo takes place in measures 49–80. Blues licks dominate the beginning of each A section, while most of the activity in the B sections involves chord outlining. Noteworthy are the humorous imitative sequence in measures 57–60 and the long, continuous triplet phrase in measures 69–77. In the latter, the articulation pattern of downstroke-upstroke-downstroke for each triplet is recommended. The octave solo returns to the head in measure 81; the first half is in single notes while the second is in octaves. This leads to a riff-based six-bar tag and the closing free-time ending. Here Montgomery concludes the piece with a unique dissonance: Dm(maj7add11)/B for a mysterioso effect.

5 Fig. 3

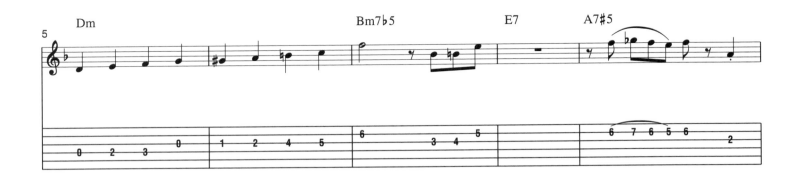

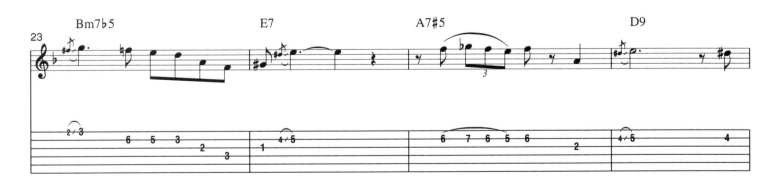

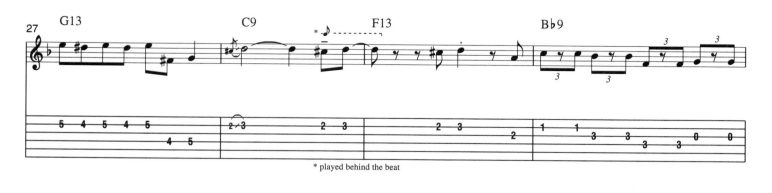

* played behind the beat

Guitar Solo

A 1st Chorus

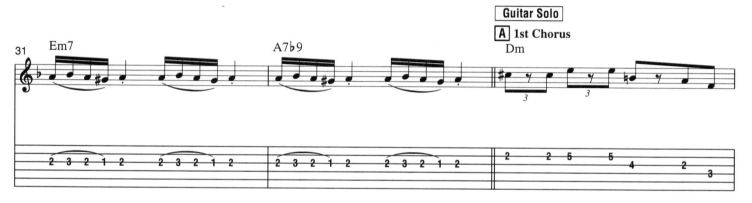

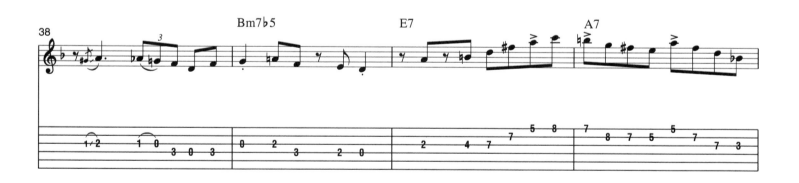

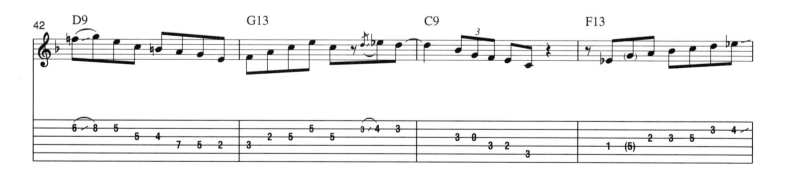

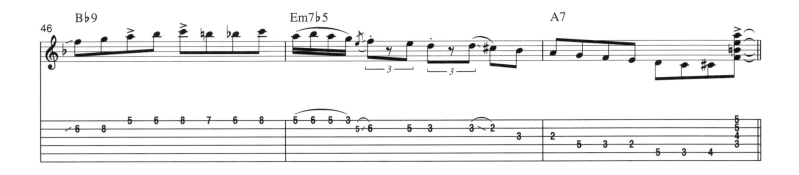

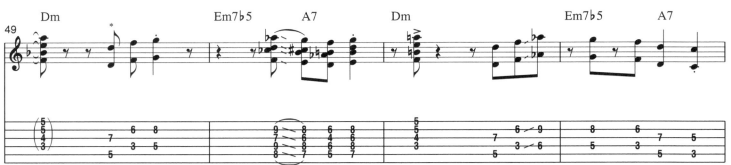

* Mute inner string of octaves throughout.

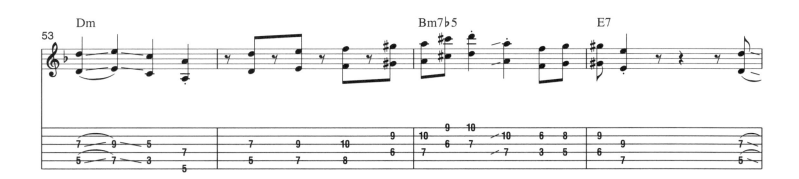

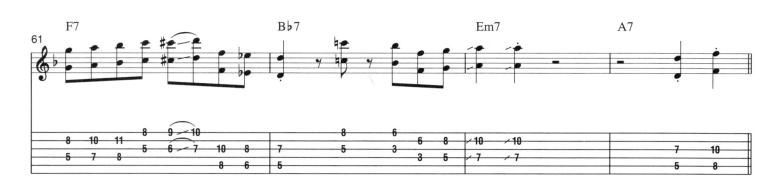

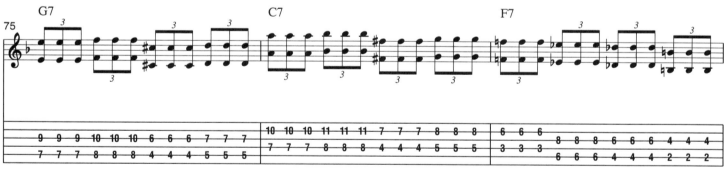

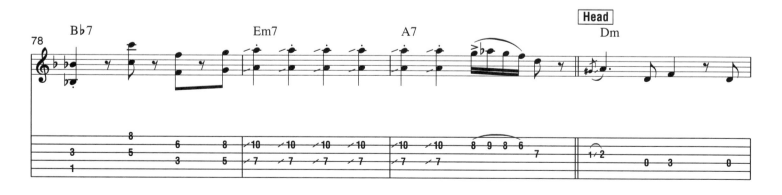

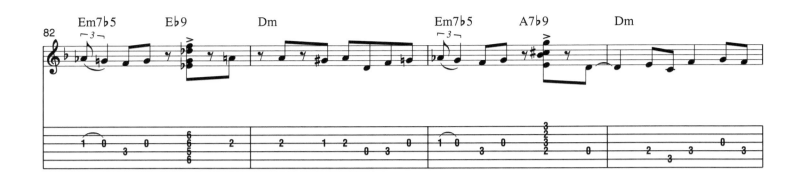

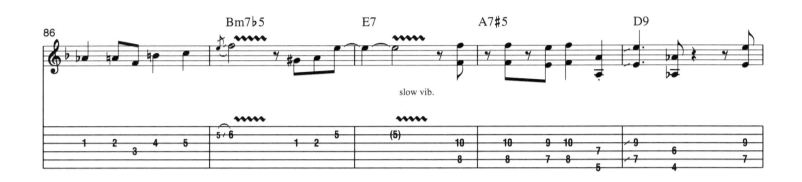

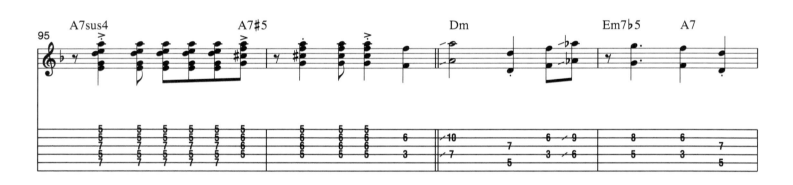

WEST COAST BLUES
(The Incredible Jazz Guitar of Wes Montgomery)
By John L. (Wes) Montgomery

Figure 4—Head and Solo

Montgomery's sophomore effort, 1960's *The Incredible Jazz Guitar of Wes Montgomery,* rightfully earned him a slew of accolades and established his talent in the jazz community. The ensemble was a quartet: Tommy Flanagan (piano), Percy Heath (bass), and Tootie Heath (drums), led by Montgomery. A highlight of the record was his original composition "West Coast Blues," which has since become a standard. Fresh and infectious, it is a loping 6/4 blues in B♭ with "West Coast changes" and a relaxed jazz-waltz feel.

The head is built on a catchy Mixolydian riff introduced in the first measure and taken thematically through the blues form. Note the familiar Montgomery chromatic twist in measure 4. Here he inserts a substitute for B♭7, a Bm7–E7 change, into the blues progression. The riff is rejoined and altered melodically to fit E♭7 in measures 5–6. In measures 9–10 Montgomery employs a secondary riff over the V and IV chords. Note the motivic similarity on beats 3 and 4 of each measure of this riff to the substitute figure of measure 4.

Wes Montgomery's solo in "West Coast Blues" is played over nine choruses of B♭ blues. It features a more animated swing feel and uses his signature three-tier improvisation strategy. The first four choruses are in single notes, choruses 5, 6, and 7 are in octaves, and the final two are played in block chords. His lines indicate that he is responding to the alternate changes of the progression: A♭7 in measure 2, Bm7–E7 in measure 4, E♭m7–A♭7 in measure 6, the ii–V changes in measures 7–10, and the B♭maj7–D♭7–G♭maj7–B7 turnaround in measures 11–12.

Montgomery's single-note solo is played predominately in eighth-note rhythm units, endemic to the swing-based bebop style. His phrasing and time are impeccable throughout. Strong blues ideas abound, most notably in measures 1, 25, 29–30, 34–35, 37, and 46–47. Finger vibrato, string bending, and use of the B♭ minor pentatonic and blues scales in the third chorus, measures 29–30, further illustrate Montgomery's earthier side. Good examples of his motivic development are found in measures 14–16 and 21–22. In the latter phrase, Montgomery expounds on a motive made of a lower-neighbor-tone figure and a descending arpeggio, somewhat like the bridge of "Take Five." Measure 37 contains a bluesy quote from Charlie Christian, Montgomery's early role model. The attractive question and answer phrase in measures 39–40 is a another laudable highlight.

Montgomery's octave choruses elaborate on his single-note lines. Notable portions include the descending sequence in measure 53 and the energetic rhythmic activity of measures 60–63. The latter features an octave jump—in octaves! Measures 69–70 contain an unmistakable Montgomery signature lick which melds two familiar elements: a rising Cm11 (C–E♭–G–B♭–D–F) arpeggio decorated with lower neighbor notes (B, D, F♯, A, C♯, E) followed by a down-home melody utilizing the B♭ blues scale (B♭–D♭–E♭–E–F–A♭). An interesting rhythmically-displaced version of this lick occurs in measures 81–82. Riff-based melodies are exploited in measures 73–75.

Montgomery takes the final two choruses in block chords. His opening phrases in both choruses are strong and funky, and exemplify his horn-section thinking applied to guitar. Note the use of chromatic motion in the form of passing chords (measures 85–86, 91–92, and 94) and his signature "push chords" which approach the primary chords of the progression from either a half step below or above. Each individual chord phrase is worthy of extraction and study, as it is fascinating and instructive to see how Montgomery handled the individual sections of the blues form harmonically. Highlights include the numerous ii–V patterns and their variants (measures 88, 90–94, 102–106), the augmented chord substitutions in measure 100, and Montgomery's treatment of the turnarounds in measures 95–96 and 107–108.

6 Fig. 4

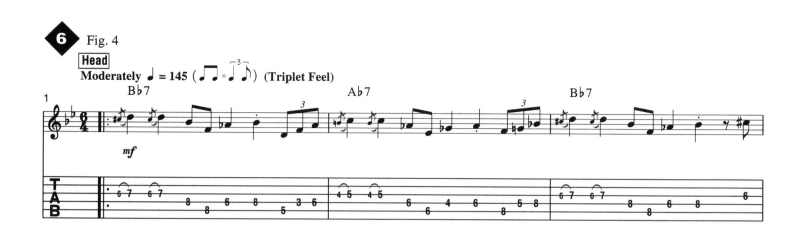

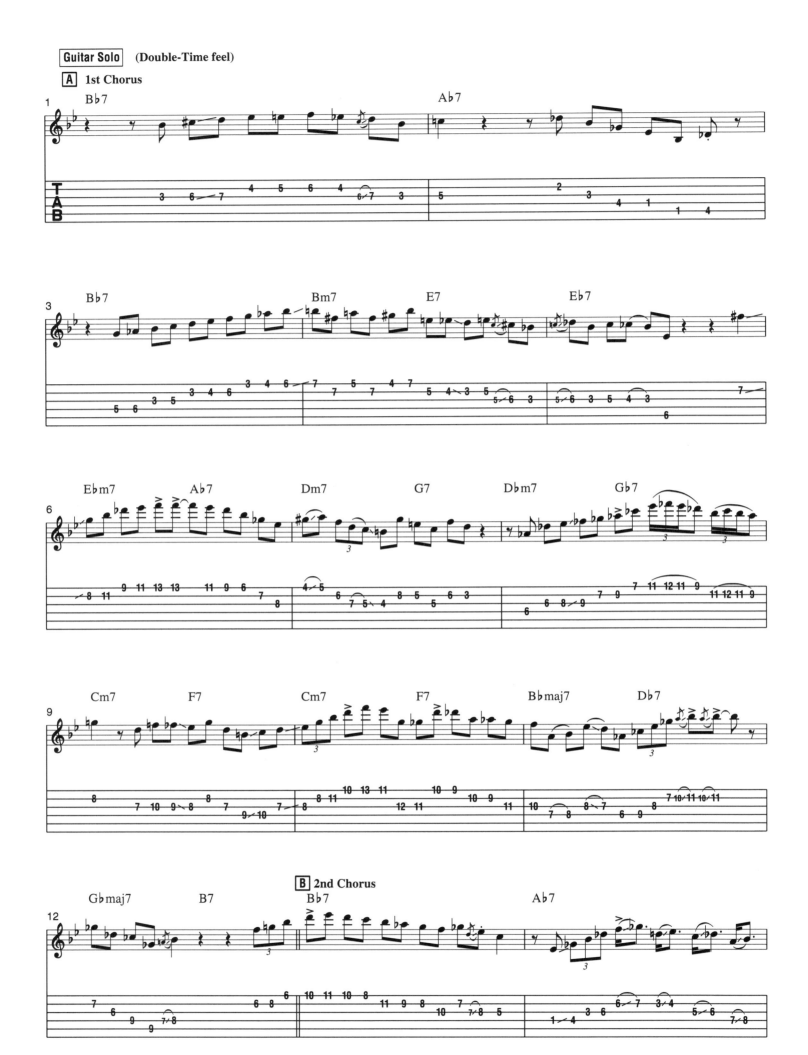

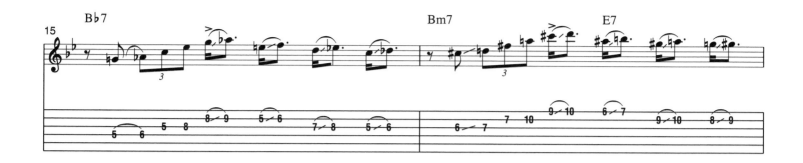

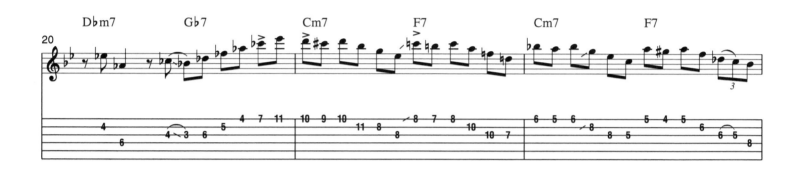

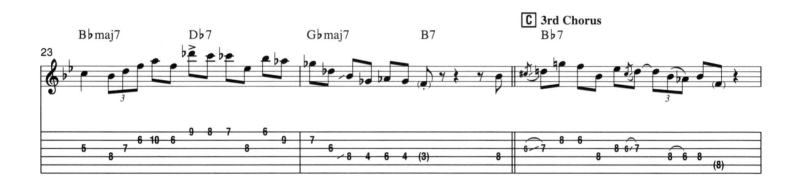

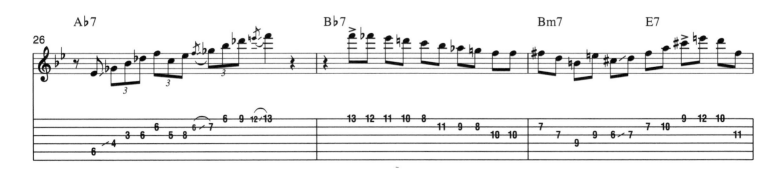

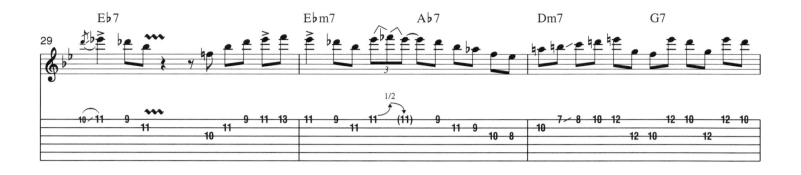

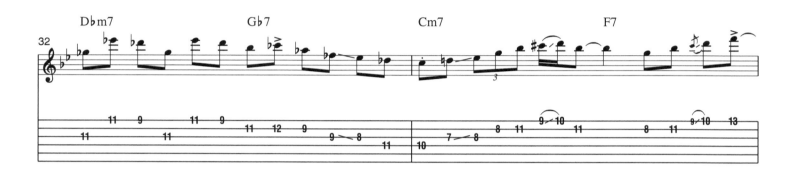

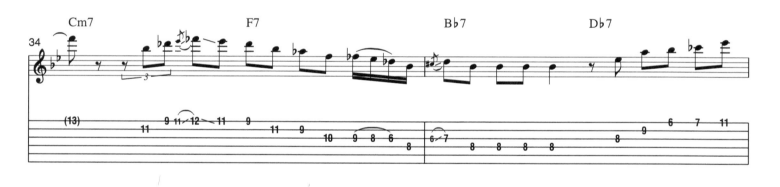

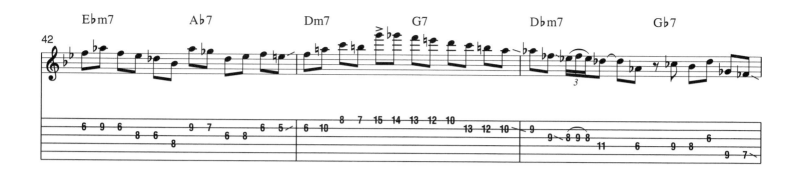

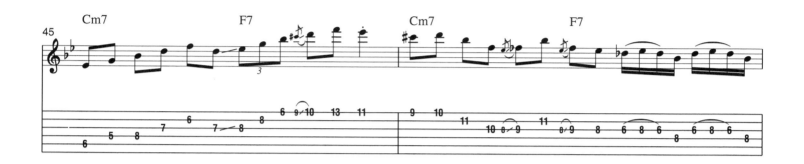

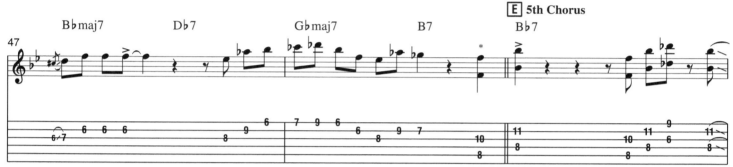

E 5th Chorus

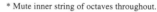

* Mute inner string of octaves throughout.

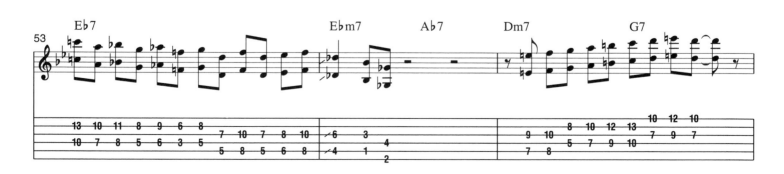

29

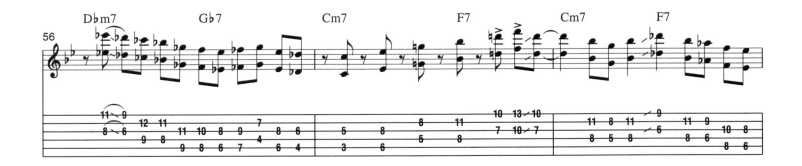

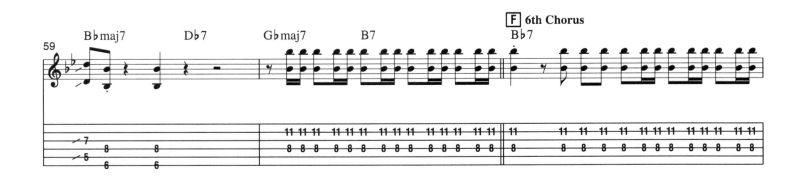

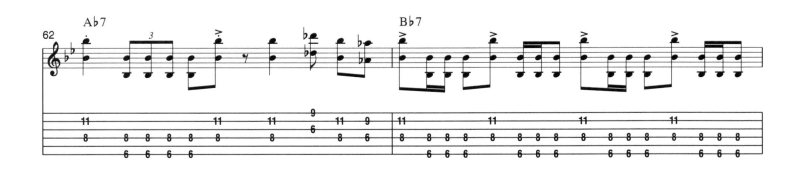

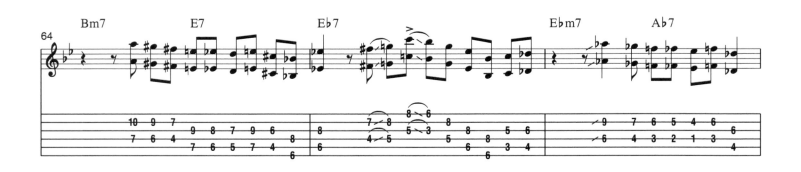

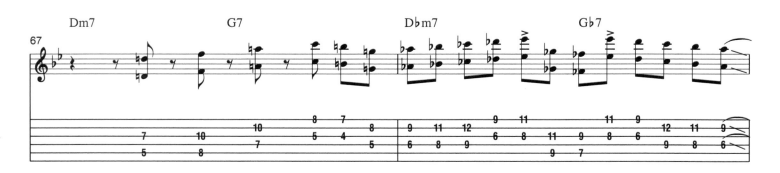

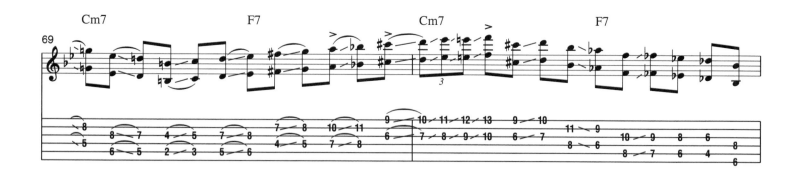

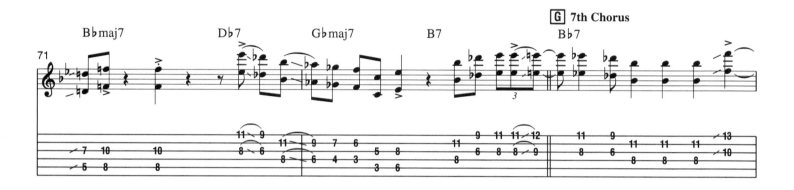

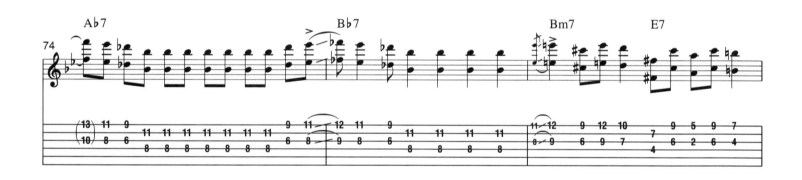

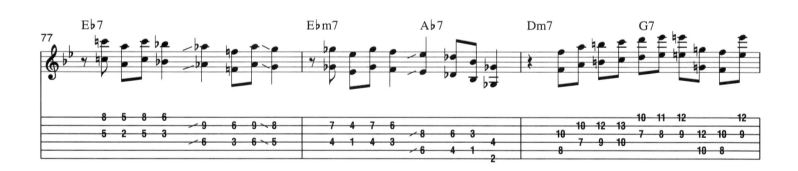

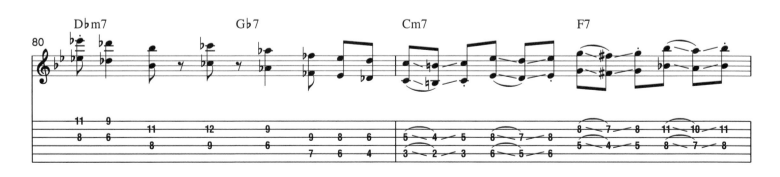

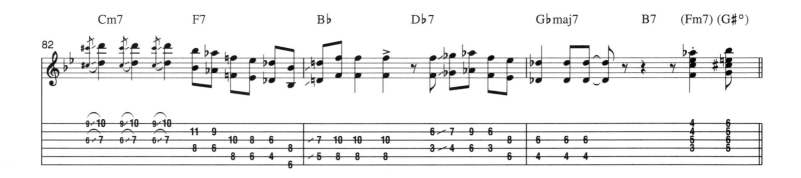

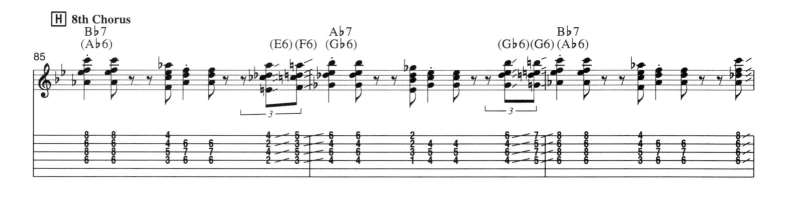

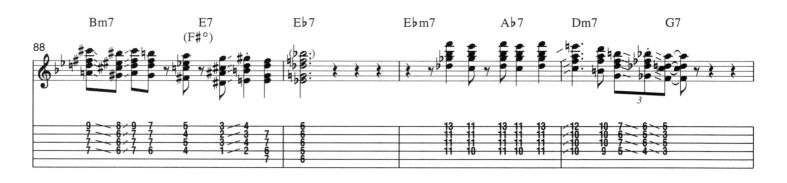

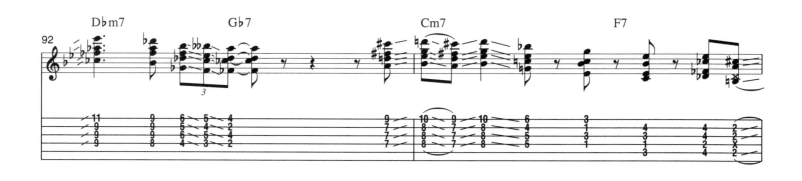

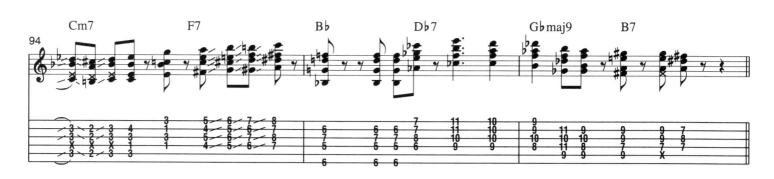

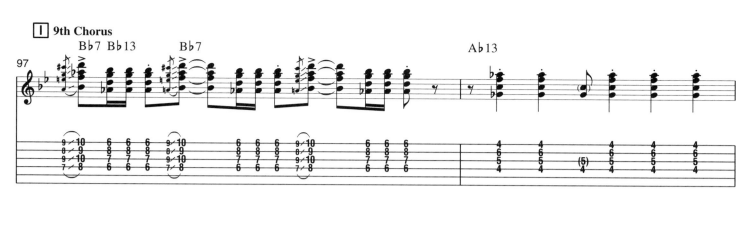

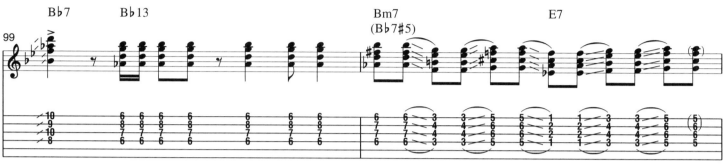

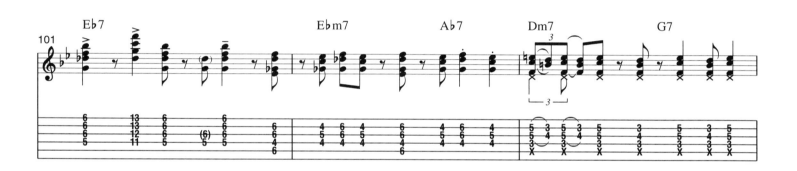

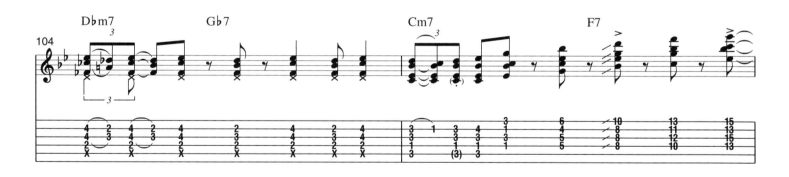

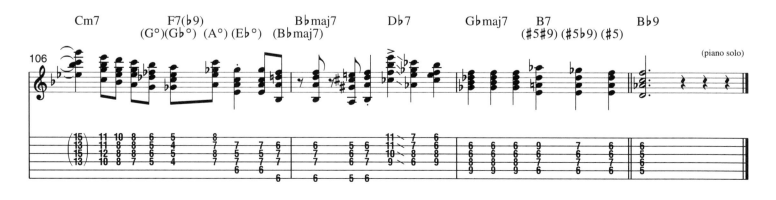

CARIBA
(Full House)
By John L. (Wes) Montgomery

Figure 5—Head

In 1962 Wes Montgomery recorded an album which was a career milestone. *Full House* was captured live at Tsubo's Coffee House in Berkeley, CA—chosen for its ambiance and acoustics. Montgomery secured the Miles Davis rhythm section (Wynton Kelly, Paul Chambers, and Jimmy Cobb) for the dates and augmented the lineup with Johnny Griffin on tenor sax. A high point of the sessions was the Montgomery original "Cariba." A spirited 12-bar blues set in an Afro-Cuban groove, it contains a colorful and characteristically twisted head and one of his most aggressive solos.

The head—though straightforward, riff-dominated and one of Montgomery's simplest compositions—exploits unusual elements. It is in essence a modal blues. The basic riff played on the B♭7 and E♭7 (I and IV changes) is rendered as a series of inverted minor-seventh chords (Fm7 and B♭m7) in measures 1–7. Montgomery states these riffs in block chords. The F13 and E♭13 V–IV progression in measures 8–10 exploits block chords with octave breaks as a secondary riff. Note the approach to the V chord via an Fm7–G♭9–F13 passage. The approach from a half step above is a harmonic trademark found in numerous Montgomery chord phrases.

* Mute inner string of octaves throughout.

Figure 6—Solo

The "Cariba" solo is one of Montgomery's finest and funkiest. It occurs over eleven choruses of a B♭ blues with a groove so driving it borders on Latin rock. Appropriately, he begins each chorus with a riff-oriented idea, starting with a rhythmic phrase emphasizing repeated notes. The repeated-note motive is maintained through the solo choruses and reappears in many varied forms. Montgomery's single-note phrases in the first three choruses A – C make use of pentatonic sounds, and are remarkably rhythmic and riff-oriented in contrast to the bop-based lines of other blues solos in his repertory. Signature Montgomery licks are found in measures 7, 11, 20–23 and 30–32.

Solo choruses 4–8 D – H are splendid examples of Montgomery's octave style. Generally, his octave phrases stick with the riff-based, rhythmic format established in the single-note choruses. Most of his phrases are based on pentatonic and blues melodies or diatonic arpeggios. A notable exception is the use of the Bm9 arpeggio (B–D–F♯–A–C♯) melody in measure 40. This functions as a half-step-above approach to the B♭m9 melody in measures 41–42, and is a typical Montgomery maneuver. Also noteworthy is the strong off-beat descending passage in measures 73–76. Though it is played in steady eighth-note rhythm, Montgomery creates an emphatic internal syncopation by accenting the weak parts of each beat and slurring into the strong beats. He mixes octaves and chords in the ninth chorus I , building toward a powerful funky climax in the tenth chorus which is played entirely in block chords. Montgomery returns to octaves and chords to close the solo in measures 129–132. He rejoins the head melody at the solo's conclusion in measure 133.

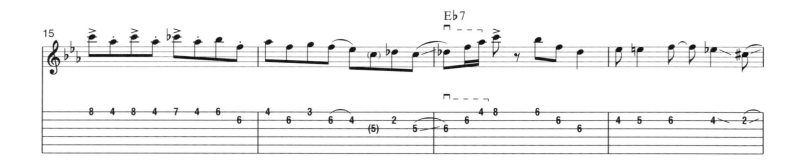

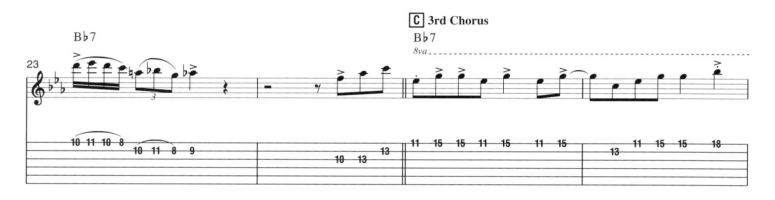

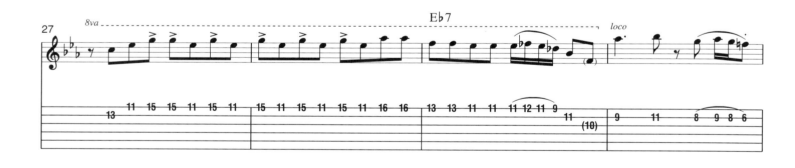

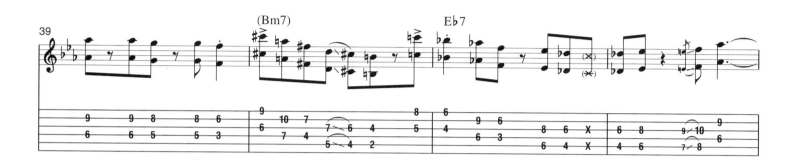

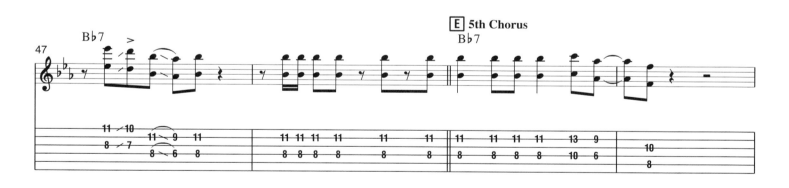
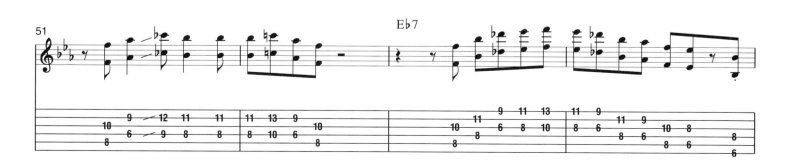

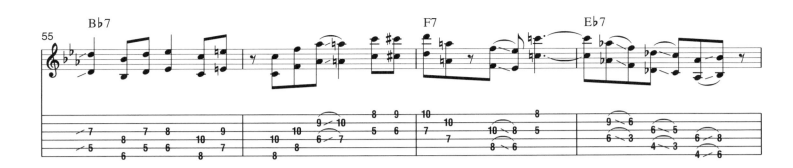

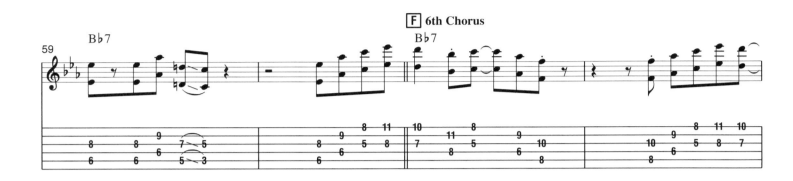

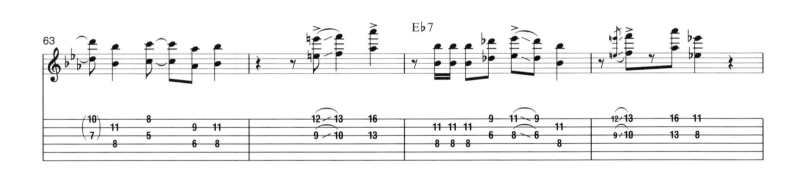

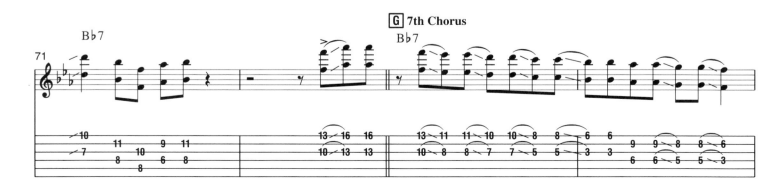

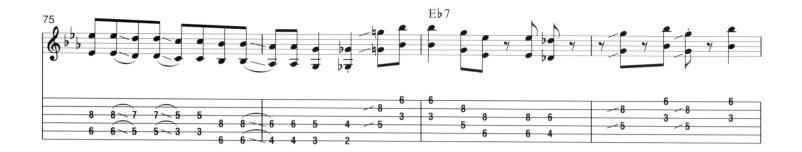

H 8th Chorus

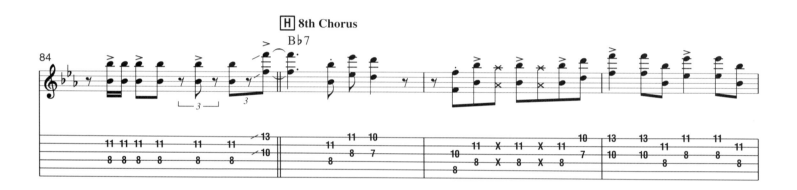

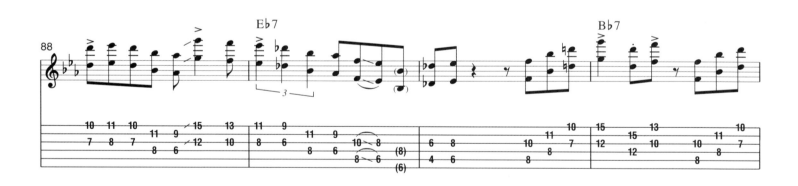

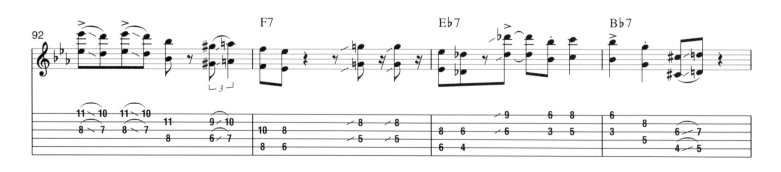

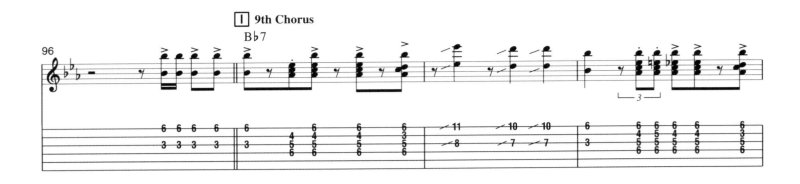

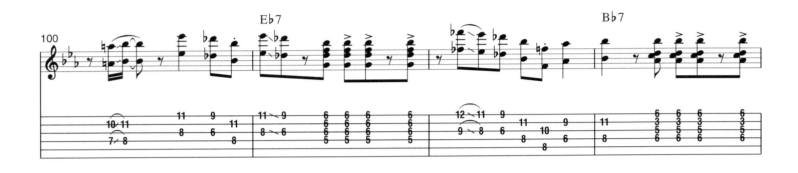

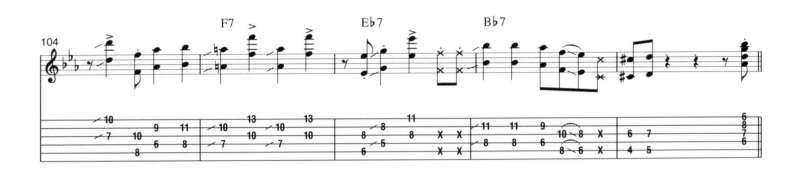

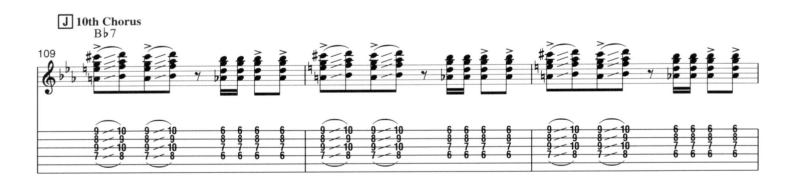

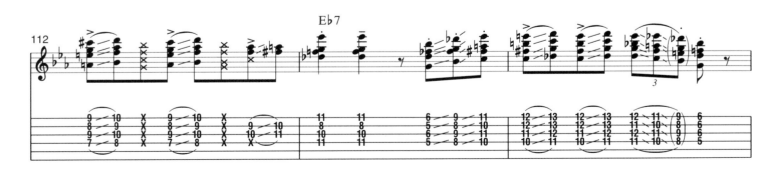

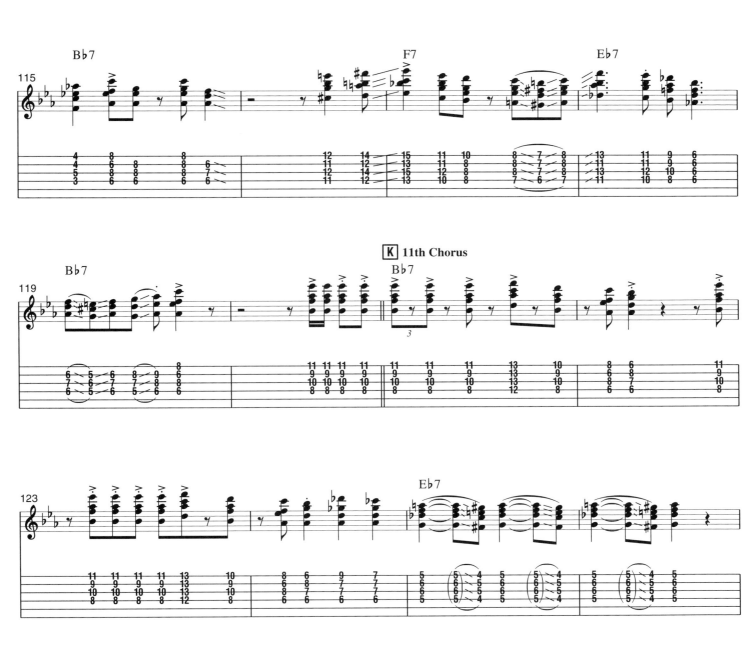

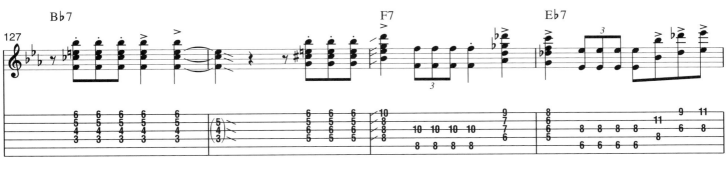

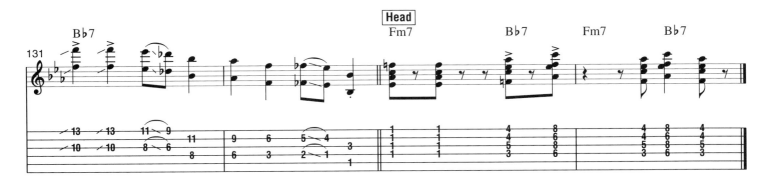

I'VE GROWN ACCUSTOMED TO HER FACE
from MY FAIR LADY
(Full House)

Words by Alan Jay Lerner
Music by Frederick Loewe

Figure 7—Intro

"I've Grown Accustomed to Her Face," which was also recorded in the Tsubo concerts, showcases another aspect of Wes Montgomery's artistry: his chord melody style. This gorgeous ballad finds him in a soft trio setting, playing his arrangement of the Lerner-Loewe standard gently and introspectively. Light accompaniment is supplied only by upright bass and drums (with brushes).

Montgomery's arrangement begins in a distinctive Spanish mood with an atypical, unaccompanied eight-bar intro played rubato. He poses E, F, D, and Am6 chords over a low E pedal point for a strong ethnic effect. This seemingly incongruent opening leads seamlessly to a chord-melody rendering of the tune in measure 8. Here the E tonal center becomes the V of V (A7) to modulate into D major.

9 Fig. 7

Intro
Moderately Slow ♩ = ca 76-80
Rubato (Free Time)

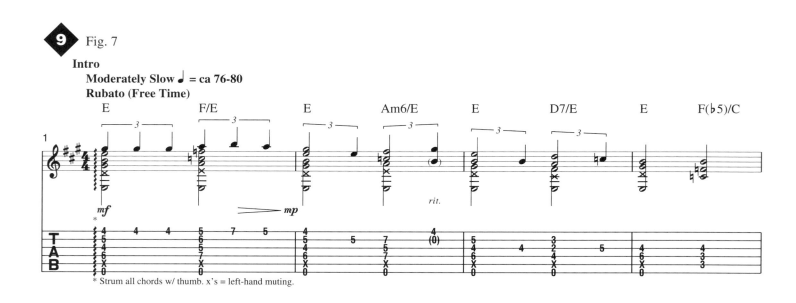

* Strum all chords w/ thumb. x's = left-hand muting.

A Tempo

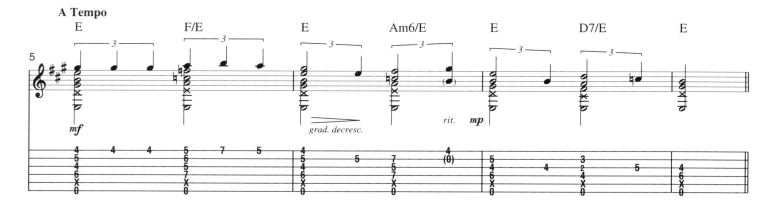

Figure 8—Head, Interlude, Recap, and Outro

The actual tune begins in measure 9 [A] and is played in D with the rhythm section. Montgomery states the melody in chords with tasteful reharmonizations throughout, striking a balance between diatonic, chromatic, and modal harmony. Note his characteristic diminished chords used to harmonize parts of the theme melody in measures 8, 10, and 13–16. A four-bar interlude [B] is played unaccompanied and provides a wonderful harmonic surprise in the F#m7–Dm7–Amaj9 progression. [C] is a return to an abbreviated version of the song's melody, the second half of the tune's form. The piece closes with a recap [D] of Montgomery's Spanish intro. Noteworthy is the unique penultimate chord, Dm6/E, in measure 51. This unusual wide-spread voicing was brought to my attention by my good friend, jazz guitarist Henry Johnson. Montgomery ends the piece with a lush E6/9 chord.

43

BÉSAME MUCHO (KISS ME MUCH)

(Boss Guitar)

Music and Spanish Words by Consuelo Velazquez
English Words by Sunny Skylar

Figure 9—Head and Solo

Wes Montgomery returned to the organ-trio setting for the appropriately-titled *Boss Guitar* album, recorded on April 22, 1963. Melvin Rhyne again played organ while Jimmy Cobb was in the drum chair. Amid the eight sparkling and diverse tunes was the old Latin standard "Besame Mucho," which received an uncommon arrangement as a spirited jazz waltz in B♭ minor with funk overtones. Its structure is a large AABA (32–32–16–32) song form.

After the groove is established via a i–IV7 vamp, Montgomery delivers the head melody sparsely with blues, modal (scalar and diatonic), and bebop embellishments. Blues-pentatonic cadential figures occur in measures 35–37, 66–69, and 114–117, and a slurred doublestop-and-blues lick in measures 39–40. Noteworthy is the ornamented treatment of the ascending line in measures 16–19, 48–51 ,and 96–99—which is thematic in this rendition of the melody. Also thematic are Montgomery's extemporaneous bop elaborations of the melody in measures 27–32, 59–63, and 107–113.

Montgomery's solo is played over two choruses of the song form. The first is in single notes and the second in octaves. It is highly rhythmic and—as in the head—blues, modal, and bebop elements are tastefully balanced and juxtaposed. Montgomery begins with a band-tacet break in measures 118–120 and plays shorter phrases emphasizing space until the long boppish string of eighth notes in measures 136–143. A signature blues riff is found in measures 145–152. Here, Montgomery produces a call-and-response effect by alternating blues licks with a recurring slurred double stop. The sequential phrase in measures 161–165 exemplifies his deft motivic development of simple scale melodies. This culminates in a striking bebop line in measures 166–167, containing chromaticism and its own internal thematic development with a repeated F pedal tone. The bridge is dominated by blues riffs in measures 185–195. Throughout his improvisations, Montgomery employs a particular figure incorporating a series of staggered eighth notes, as in measures 143–144, 151–152, 178–179, 227–228, 253–256, and 335–336. This syncopation acts as a strong and unifying rhythmic agent in the phrases.

Montgomery's octave solo contains numerous highlights. The blues-oriented sounds cultivated in the first chorus also dominate this chorus, particularly in important cadences. Strong melodic riffs are heard in the question-and-answer phrases of measures 240–248 and 281–288. A classic slurred-octave articulation occurs in measures 289–292. An ear-catching rhythmic motive is introduced and developed in the bridge: measures 297–310. This is based on the repetition of a one-and-a-half-beat pattern (two eighths and an eighth rest) and is characteristic of another group of Montgomery motives which create syncopation by accenting, use of rests, and metric placement. The melodic content in this section is primarily made of arpeggios. In measures 320–328 Montgomery produces a compelling rhythmic episode involving a repeated eighth-note triplet and quarter-note figure. Note the hemiola effect created by the rhythmic displacement of the two-beat figures within the song's 3/4 meter. Note also the larger groupings in two-bar phrases in measures 323–328. This is motivic development occurring on two levels simultaneously and is an indicator of Montgomery's natural improvising genius. Moments such as this abound in his music.

Fig. 9

Intro

Cut-Time Latin Waltz ♩. = 66-70 (♪♪ = ♪ ♪) **Triplet Feel**

* Mute inner string of octaves throughout.

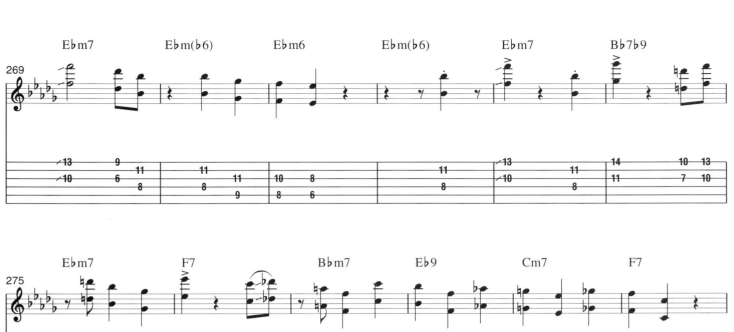

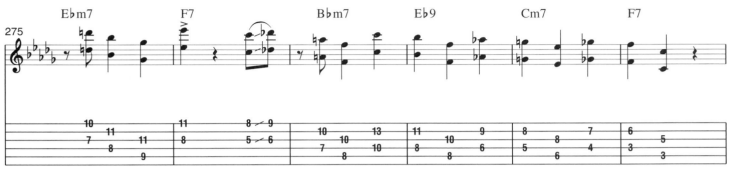

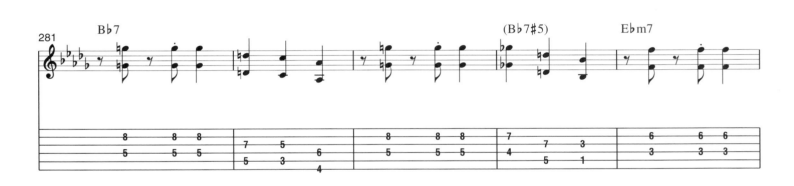

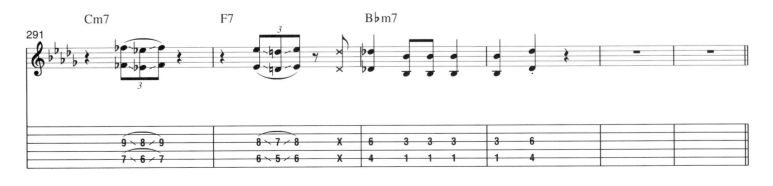

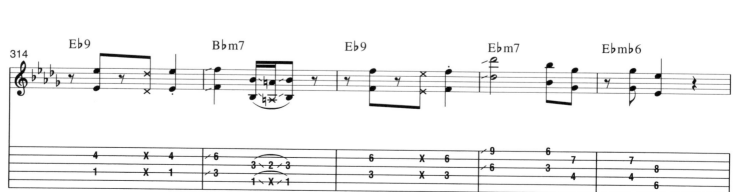

FRIED PIES
(Boss Guitar)
By John L. (Wes) Montgomery

Figure 10—Head

"Fried Pies" was regarded in *Downbeat's* review of the *Boss Guitar* album as a "cooking, horizontally-stretched blues," and that's as succinct and apt a description as may be found anywhere. It is a beloved Montgomery composition and one of his most memorable efforts in the organ-trio genre. An uncommon 12-bar blues in F, the tune features a clever arrangement with a tricky ensemble line in the head, a two-part structure for improvisations with a harmonic departure and a feel change, and an exemplary guitar solo—one of his best.

The head juggles brisk single-note blues figures with accented, off-beat chord jabs. These phrases are played in lock-step by the guitar and organ. The 12-bar format and its customary progressions are more implied than overtly stated in the head. Note the unusual placements of the I and IV chords (F7 and Bb7). Measures 8–9 contain a characteristic Montgomery mutation of the blues changes with tritone substitutions: Ab13 for D7, Db9 for Gm7, and B13 for F7. The turnaround in measures 11–12 employs a subtle harmonic twist. Here, the usual progression is supplanted with an Am7–D7–G7–C7 progression that maintains an F note as the top voice through the chord changes. This pedal note creates the raised 5th, raised 9th, and suspended 4th dissonances in the progression. The strong rhythmic element, always present in Montgomery's compositions, is found in the purposeful syncopation on the "and" of beat 2 in measures 2–8 and the off-beat punches in measures 9 and 11. Measure 10 contains a familiar blues-scale cadential line: a soulful cliché that is neatly inserted into the uncommon Montgomery melody.

Fig. 10

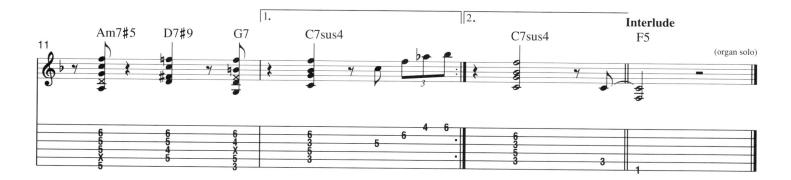

Figure 11—Solo

Montgomery's solo is a landmark outing. The first section, measures 1–16, is an interlude which occurs over a droning F5 chord in half-time feel. Montgomery plays modally for the most part, mixing minor and dominant-seventh melodies tastefully. The opening phrase in measure 2 is a minor mode line which cadences on, and then emphasizes, through repetition, the C♭ (flatted 5th) blue note. He switches tonalities to the major/dominant side in measures 8–14. Here his lines clearly favor the major third (A). The descending triplet lick in measures 13–14 is pure F major pentatonic (F–G–A–C–D).

An accented C7♯5(♯9)–F13 change brings in the second part of the solo. This is set in a more traditional but cooking swing feel and played as multiple choruses of a 12-bar blues in F. His opening six-bar phrase is a gem which lends a bebop air to the proceedings from the outset. Note the distinctive chromaticism, interval jumps, mix of arpeggio and scale melody, and feeling of resolution in the line. By contrast, Montgomery latches onto a swinging, riff-oriented blues line in measures 23–28. Bebop phrases dominate the second chorus B from the fourth measure. The cadential lick in measure 32 is one of his favorite melodic patterns, found in varied forms in many solos. The florid, horn-influenced flurry in measures 36–38 is the sort of line that left countless listeners astounded at Montgomery's technical prowess with the thumb. The double-timed melody is in G minor, incorporates the flatted 5th (D♭), and employs arpeggio and scalar contours. Note the deliberate interval skips Montgomery leaves in the scale passages of measure 37 and the raked articulation in measure 38. The ending of the phrase in measure 39 is a solid blues cadential melody. The third chorus C is marked by a definite blues bent. Riff ideas abound in measures 41–43 and measures 48–52, punctuated by a variation of a favorite bop cadential line in measure 44. Montgomery introduces a thematic slurred double stop in measure 48 which is developed in the ensuing seven measures. Note that only one note (G♯–A) is slurred in this double stop. The D is maintained above as a pedal tone. The blues bent is continued into the fourth chorus D. In measures 60–64, an attractive swinging blues riff built on a repeated D pushes toward the final single-note chorus. The fifth chorus E is the climax of the single-note solo. It exploits a playful Montgomery motive of hammered, descending scale licks which is sequenced and adjusted to fit the backing chords—most notably the remote B7 in measure 68, a favorite harmonic substitution. Measures 71–75 contain reinterpreted blues clichés which provide a beautiful earthy closure to the section.

Choruses F – I are superb examples of Montgomery's octave soloing in a straight-ahead blues context. Here, as in the single-note solos, he balances bebop melodies with groove-oriented blues riffs that generally begin each chorus. The phrase in measures 89–93 is exemplary. Note Montgomery's progression from a descending series of call-and-response riffs in four registers to an angular cadential bop lick. The latter makes use of 9th, 13th, raised 5th, and flatted 9th tones. This signature Montgomery cadential line is heard again in varied form in measures 113–117.

*Played ahead of the beat.

*Played behind the beat.

B 2nd Chorus

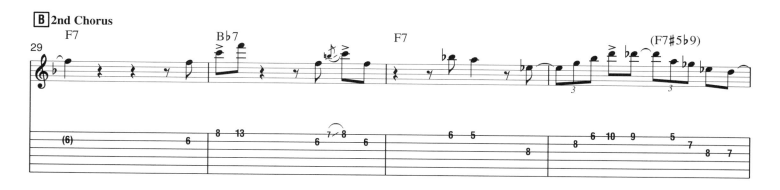

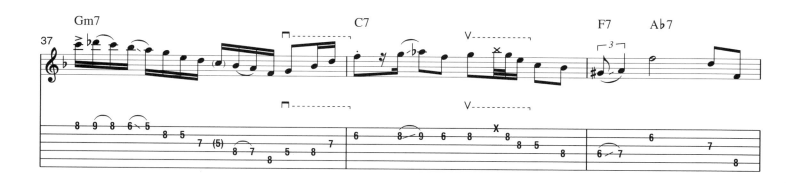

E 5th Chorus

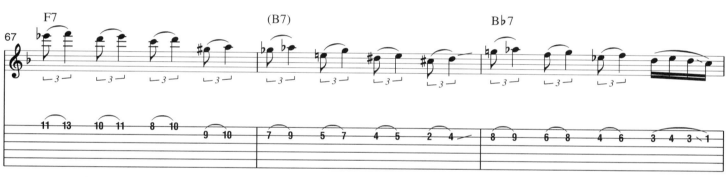

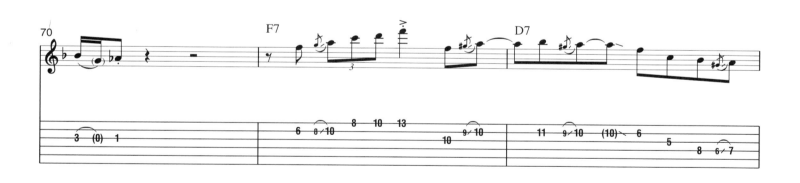

*Mute inner string of octaves throughout.

9th Chorus

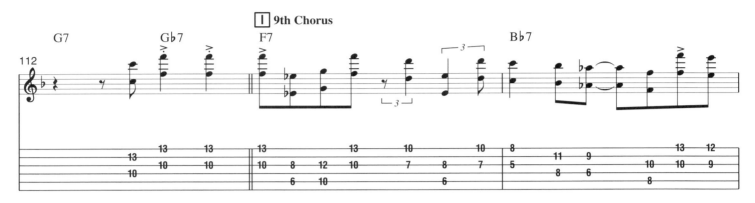

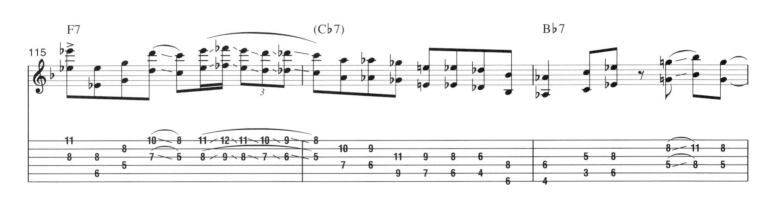

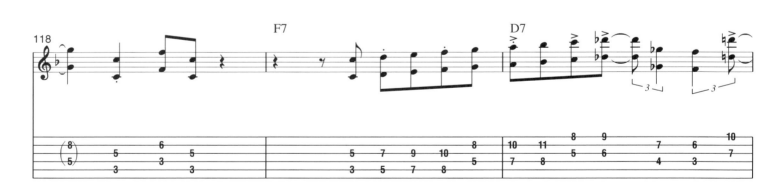

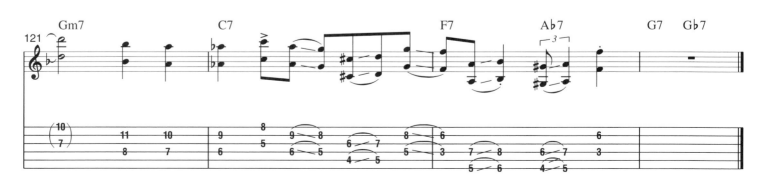

MI COSA
(Guitar on the Go)
By John L. (Wes) Montgomery

Figure 12

This beautiful chord solo was unavailable for many years. Originally scheduled for Wes Montgomery's last Riverside album *Guitar on the Go*, it only appeared on OJC reissues. The track was recorded on October 10, 1963, without a title, labeled "unidentified solo guitar," and shelved for over twenty years. It came to be known as "Mi Cosa" ("My Thing" in Spanish). A full-scale version with Don Sebesky's Orchestra was later recorded for Verve in 1965. The earlier Riverside version was Montgomery's only unaccompanied chord solo on an original composition, and stands as one of his finest moments in the catalog. It offers much that is associated with the Montgomery chord style: colorful, modern jazz voicings, lush, widely-voiced impressionistic harmonies, romantic Spanish-Moorish overtones, and bittersweet dissonances, delivered with the unmistakable thick tone and singular touch of his thumb attack.

"Mi Cosa" is a sectional piece which sounds partially improvised. It begins with a brooding, suspended intro that poses dissonant chords like B♭add♯4, B/A, Bm7♭5, and A7♭9(♯11) over an A pedal point. The B♭-to-A chord movement is emphasized and suggests a Phrygian-based Spanish atmosphere.

The main theme is introduced in measure 18. This section is pandiatonic and clearly in A major, with only momentary harmonic allusions outside the tonality in Am7 and B♭ chords. The E11, E7♯5, and Amaj13 chords are voiced as wide, open-position sonorities which lend an impressionistic quality to the theme. A second theme is found in measures 28–38. Montgomery mixes octaves and chords in this section. It features more typical jazz voicings and progressions, such as E13♭9–A6/9 and G♯7–C♯m7–F♯7♯5(♭9), as well as signature block-chord passages in measures 31–32 and 38. The second theme is reinterpreted and enlarged in measures 54–66. There, Montgomery renders the melody with his patented block chords over a sustained E pedal point. Note the emblematic use of diminished chords in the section. The coda beginning in measure 70 is a recap of the intro with a final cadence of A7♭9sus4 (Em7♭5/A)–E7♭9 (F°/E)–A.

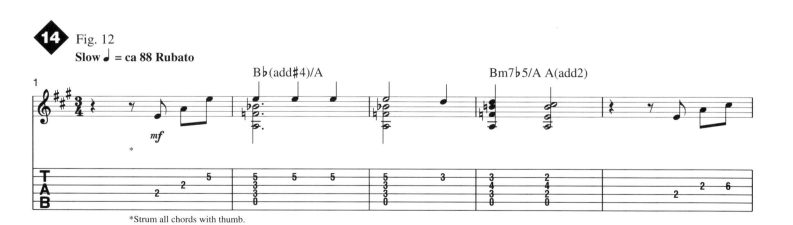

*Strum all chords with thumb.

*Mute inner string of octaves throughout.

D.S. al Coda

70

FOUR ON SIX
(Smokin' at the Half Note)
By John L. (Wes) Montgomery

Figure 13—Head and Solo

In Summer and early Fall of 1965, Wes Montgomery was recorded with the Wynton Kelly Trio in New Jersey and New York City. The resulting performances, a mixture of studio and live sessions (virtually the same thing in jazz of this era), were released by Verve Records on their *Smokin' at the Half Note* and *Willow Weep for Me* albums (and subsequently on small-group compilations) and are ranked among the finest of his career. They are the final commercially recorded, straight-ahead tunes with a working band in Montgomery's eleven-year discography. A stand-out studio track from the dates is Montgomery's original composition "Four on Six," first heard in 1960 on *The Incredible Jazz Guitar*. Like "West Coast Blues" and "O.G.D. (The Road Song)," "Four on Six" has become a standard and remained in Montgomery's repertoire throughout his career.

"Four on Six" is a straightforward piece in G minor built on a simple 16-bar ABAC (4–4–4–4) form. For this performance, it is played in the sort of uptempo (quarter note equals 202) swing groove that seems to drive the participants to greater musical heights. Its 16-bar intro is among the most recognizable and attractive in jazz. This section is distinguished by a unison, bass-register ostinato figure that is a delight to play. The line is made entirely of perfect fifths (two to a measure in fourths) which imply the backing chord progressions Gm7–C7 | Cm7–F7 | Bbm7–Eb7 | Am7–D7 | Ebm7–Ab7. Note the characteristic Montgomery elements in the uncommon ordering of the ii–V's and their chromatic motion. The head features a bouncy, four-measure modal melody in measures 17–20 and 25–28, contrasted with a well-accented sequence of ii–V changes in measures 21–24. Note the signature bebop dissonances added to these chords: the 9th to the minor seventh chords and the flatted 9th and raised 11th to the dominant chords.

Montgomery's exciting solo is played over seven choruses of the 16-bar form. The first four are in single notes, the fifth and sixth are in octaves, and block chords are added sparingly to the final chorus. Montgomery enters with a slurred-fifths figure (an allusion to the intro?) and a G minor pentatonic (G–Bb–C–D–F) lick in the pickup phrase. The majority of his lines thereafter in the A sections are based on G minor, generally the G Dorian mode (G–A–Bb–C–D–E–F). He favors extended chord and arpeggio lines in measures 33–35, 50, 57, 66–68, and 73–76, but note departures like the augmented triad arpeggios ascending in whole tones in measures 41–42. Repeated figures and riff-based improvisation occur in measures 49–52, 73–75, and most overtly in measures 81–86 and 88–94. The latter sections exploit a blues-oriented unison-interval riff that is a staple of blues guitar. The blues element is made emphatic by slurred phrasing and a soulful released string bend in measure 83. In the B and C sections, he follows the cyclical progressions by outlining the chords or moving thematic figures through the changes sequentially. Measures 36–39, 53–56, and 69–71 are telling illustrations of this approach. The turnaround (final five measures) of each chorus generally receives a bebop cadential phrase.

Montgomery's octave choruses are equally exciting. He follows a similar improvisational scheme: playing pentatonic and modal riffs and blues figures in the A sections, sequential melodies in the B sections, and bebop lines in the C sections. A highlight is the pickup and opening phrase of the last chorus (measures 126–130). Here Montgomery eludes the time, seeming to meander and upset the rhythmic equilibrium with slurred octaves, until measure 131, where he rejoins the basic pulse perfectly!—the musical equivalent of stepping off a moving escalator onto solid ground, and a remarkable moment in the solo.

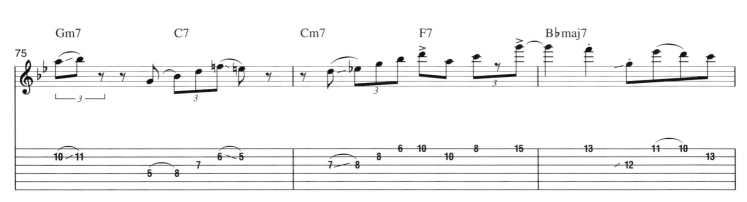

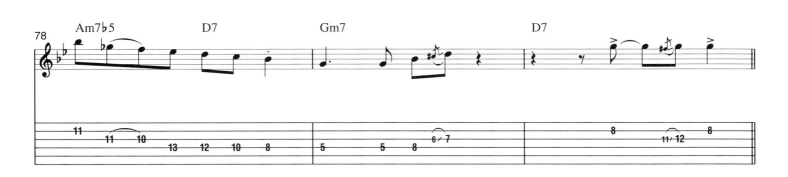

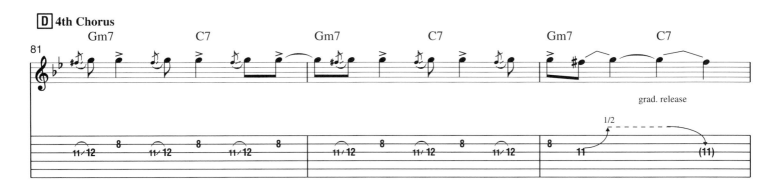

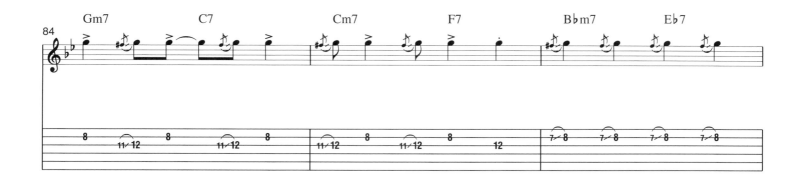

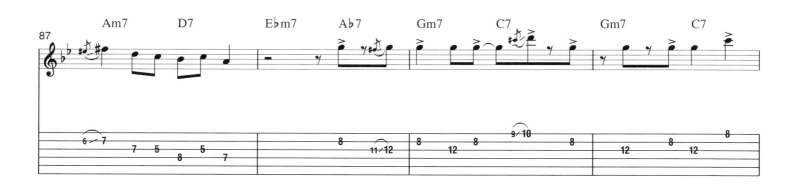

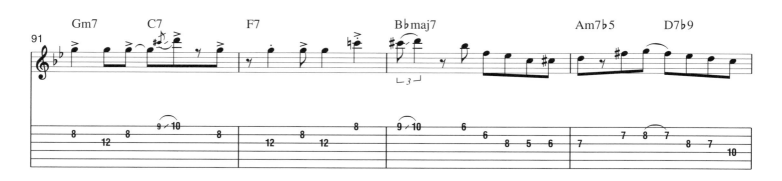

E 5th Chorus

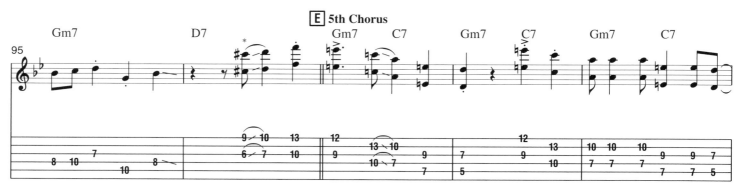

* Mute inner string of octaves throughout.

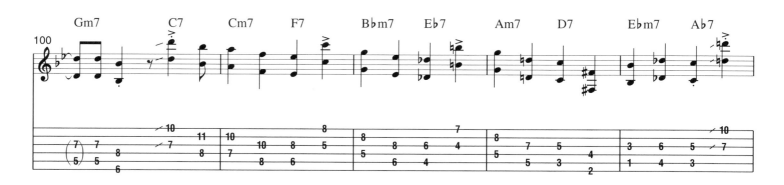

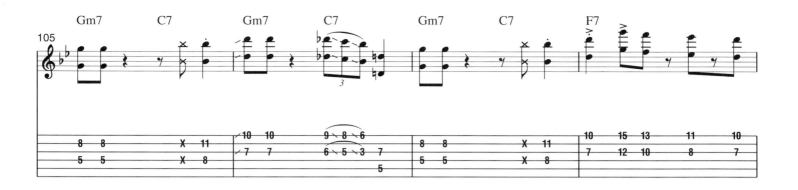

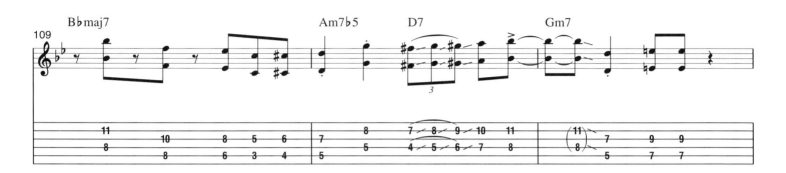

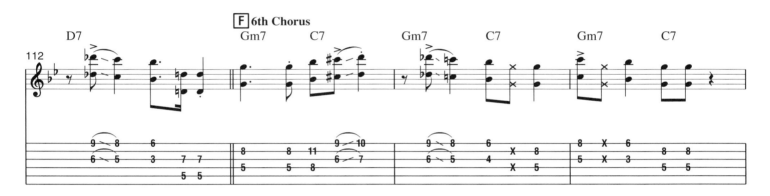

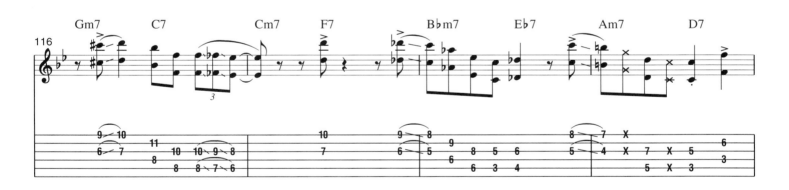

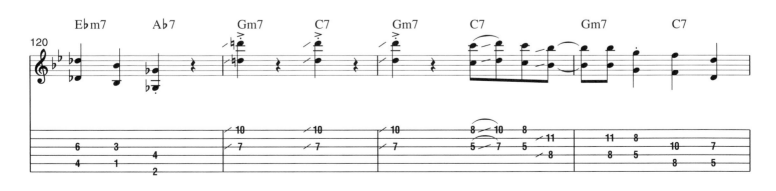

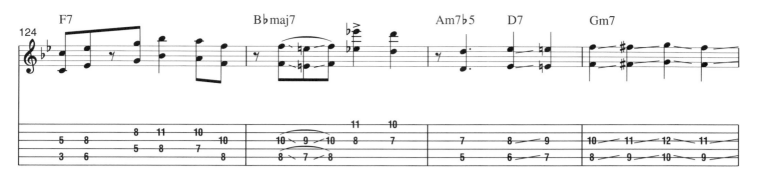

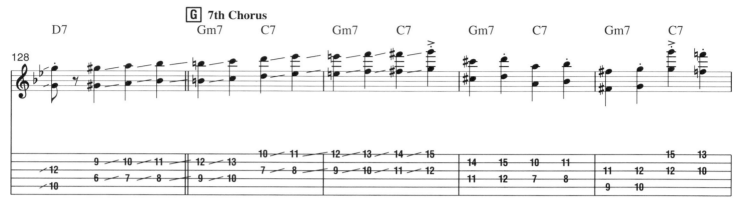

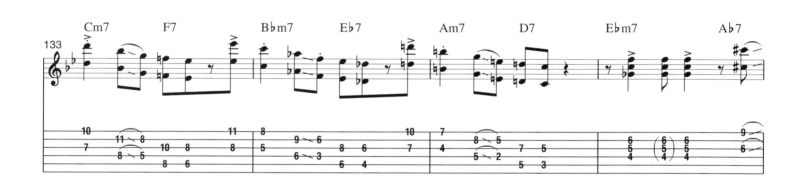

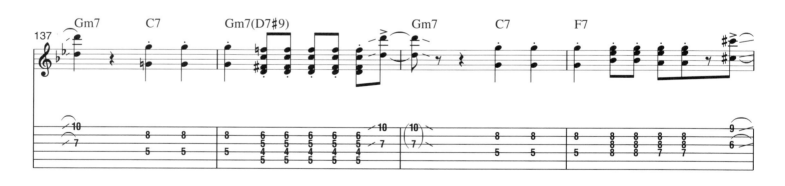

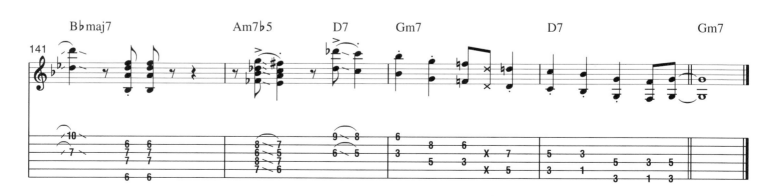

MISTY
(Willow Weep for Me)
Music by Erroll Garner

Figure 14—Head, Solo, and Outro

"Misty," Erroll Garner's beautiful standard, was recorded live in June, 1965, at the Half Note in New York City. A balladic masterpiece, it is another fortuitous result of the Wes Montgomery-Wynton Kelly Trio collaboration, and successfully captures the spirit and atmosphere of a small jazz combo performing spontaneously in a nightclub. Montgomery was the only soloist on this number, and thus it acts as a marvelous showcase for his reinterpretation and extended improvisational skills—proving that, perhaps like no other environment, the ballad setting is the ideal medium for Montgomery's wonderful nuance-filled playing. In this context his singular guitar tone is intensified, his phrasing subtleties magnified, and his rhythmic and thematic sensibilities given more room to blossom. These qualities are "beyond the page" and must be heard to be fully appreciated.

"Misty" is a 32-bar song in AABA form. Montgomery takes some liberties with the form, as is typical of ballad readings in the bebop genre. He plays the head in its entirety, solos in single notes on the complete form, jumps to the bridge for a brief octave solo, and returns to one A section of the melody and a cadenza for the outro. As in the case of Monk's "'Round Midnight" and Coltrane's "Impressions," Montgomery puts his own stamp on "Misty." He plays it in the unusual key of G (normally it is in E♭) and makes some characteristic modifications to the time-honored chord changes. These are found in the bridge (measures 23–25), where a substitute set of chords [Em9–A9–Am(maj7)–Am7♭5–A♭13] replaces the more common F♯7–A7–Bm7–E7–Am7–D7 changes seen in most fake books. The head is played in slow ballad tempo, the solos are taken with a double-time swing feel, the turnaround in the final A section is very rubato, and the cadenza is in free time, most likely conducted with visual cues.

The head is a decorated rendering of the melody. Montgomery adds a number of personal embellishments in fills and melodic connecting lines between important chord changes and in turnarounds. Highlights are: the slurred legato sequences in measures 7–9; the elegant cadential phrases in measures 15–16 and 31; the florid bebop lines in the turnaround of measures 24–25 and in the recap of the melody in measures 119–121; the bluesy ostinato of measure 29 (note the hemiola effect of his two-against-three rhythm); and the octave figures in measures 32–33.

Montgomery's solo is one of his best—beautifully crafted, melodious, and soulful. Motivic development is pursued at the outset in the imitative blues riff melodies of measures 34–37. Note how the same pitch contour is used against different chord tones: first based on the major 3rd B (for Gmaj7), then the 9th E (for Dm7) and the flatted 3rd B♭ (for an altered G7). Other significant areas of motivic development include the reprise and elaboration of his opening riff melodies over Cmaj7 and Cm7–F7 chords in measures 54–57, and the unwinding of a zigzagging triplet line over Am7–D7–Gmaj7 in measures 60–62. Bebop flurries in quick sixteenth notes are found in measures 42–44 and 72–75. Eighth-note triplet rhythm is frequently employed. Note the use of two-note and four-note pitch groups for the previously-mentioned hemiola effect in the triplet phrase of measures 86–89. The intervallic, hopping appogiatura melody in measures 51–52 is an unmistakable Montgomery signature lick, as is the bouncy descending sequence in measures 77–79. The descending line in measures 58–59 is a textbook example of the major hexatonic scale used in bebop improvisation. A blues cadential figure is worked into the improvising as an earthy touch in measures 92–94. Characteristic ostinato figures are found in measures 63, 70–72, 82–83, and 88–89. Like any gifted soloist in jazz, Montgomery always makes you feel that the song's melody is just beneath the surface of his improvisations, no matter how harmonically remote or rhythmically involved.

The outro begins with the retarding tempo in measure 124. Montgomery creates an emotional finale in octaves, tremoloing phrase endings for dramatic effect. His cadenza is played in octaves over an implied D7 chord. Note the use of the substitution melody of B major (B–D#–F#) in measure 135 which asserts a D13♭9 sound. Montgomery finishes the cadenza with a blues lick as a fanfare and a series of chromatically-descending major seventh chords in measures 136–138. His closing thoughts on the last chord are stated in an attractive octave line in measures 140–141.

Fig. 14 — Tune down (-32 cents). Slow Ballad ♩ = 54 (Rubato). Head.

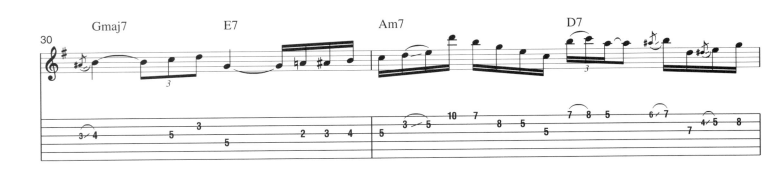

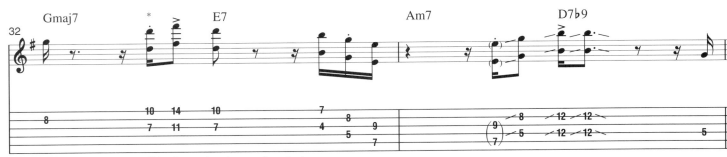

*Mute inner string of octaves throughout.

Faster ♩ = ♩ **(Double-time)** (♫ = ♩♪)

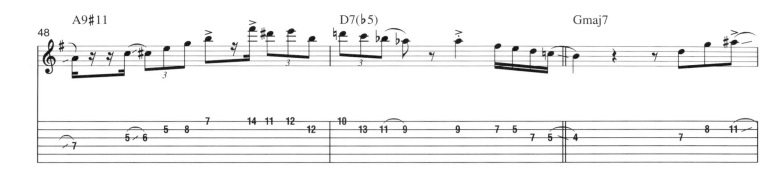

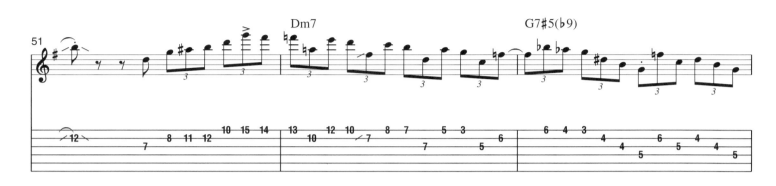

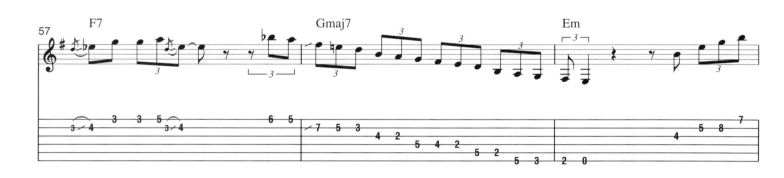

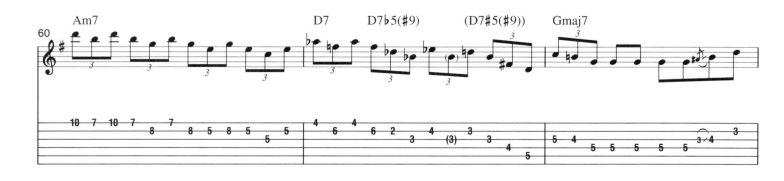

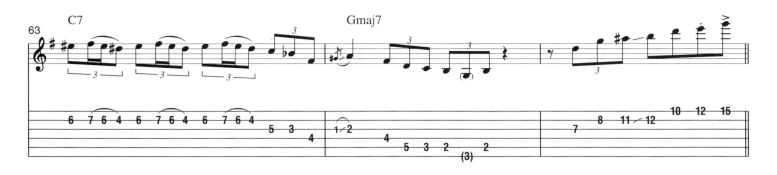

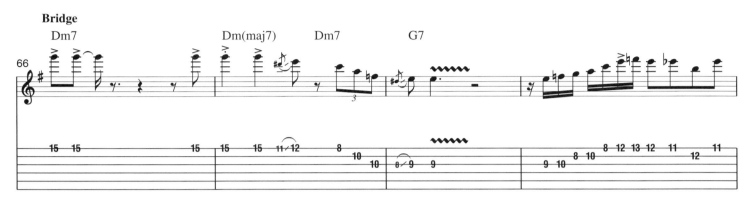

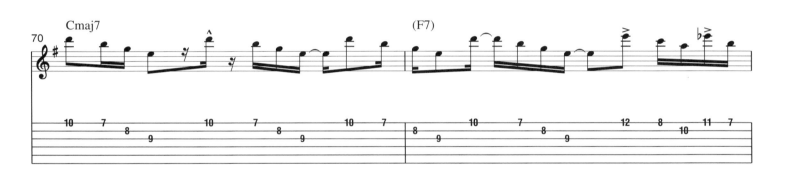

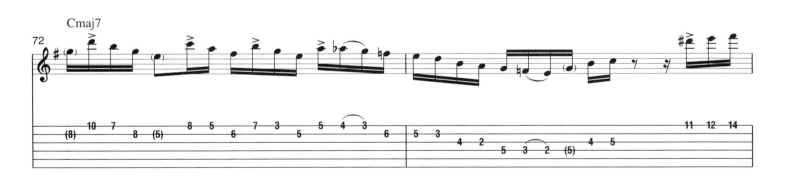

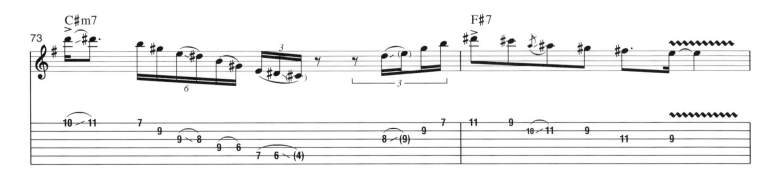

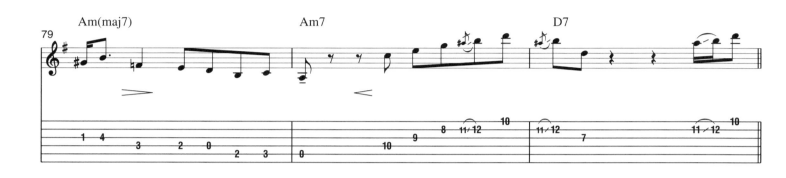

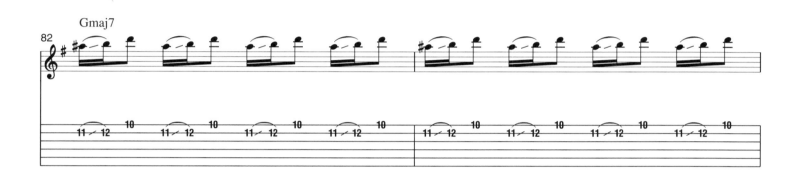

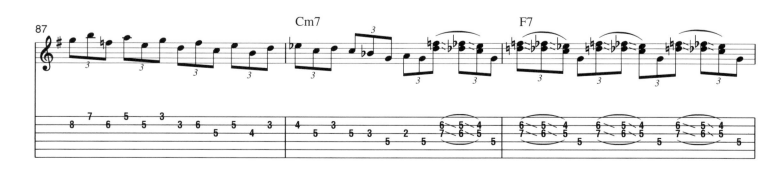

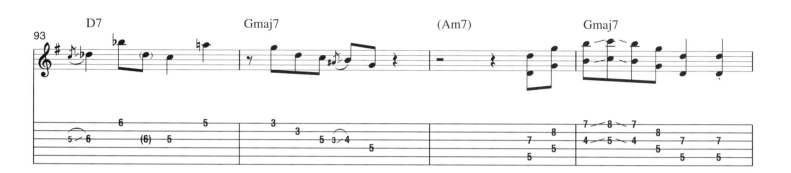

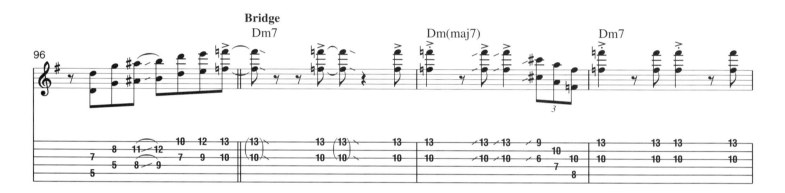

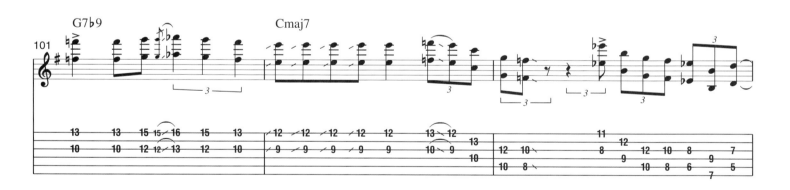

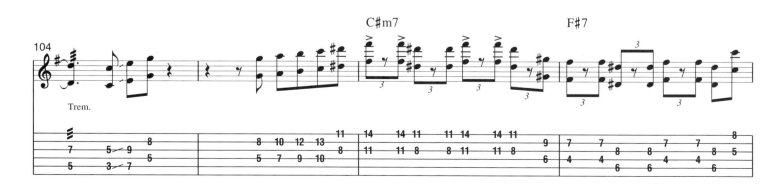

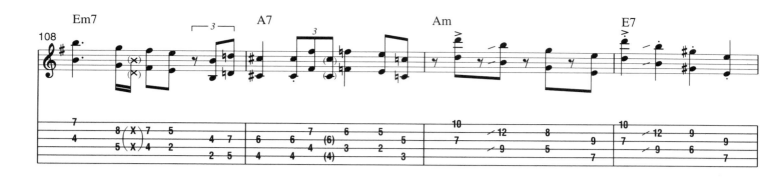

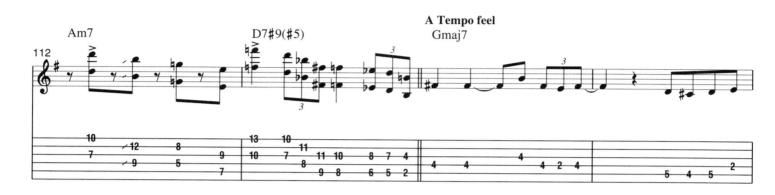

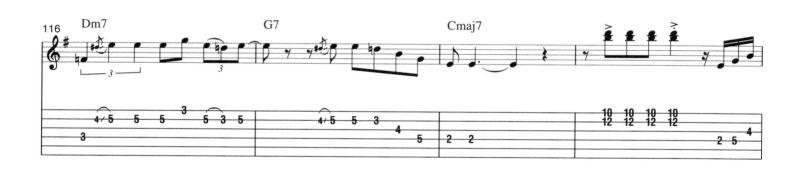

SUNDOWN
(California Dreaming)
By John L. (Wes) Montgomery

Figure 15—Head and Solo

California Dreaming was recorded in September, 1966, in the midst of Wes Montgomery's "commercial period" with Verve Records. After the chart successes of *Goin' Out of My Head* and *Tequila*, producer Creed Taylor adopted a formula of recording Montgomery with strings and horns and with a more pop-oriented repertory. Though most purists balked at the production of "trivial pop songs" in the place of bonafide jazz material, even they could not deny that the Montgomery aesthetic was still alive and kicking in occasional tracks like "Sundown." "Sundown" is an attractive Montgomery original that satisfied everyone. It is a laid-back, easy-swinging 12-bar blues in A that features the creme de la creme of the jazz scene: luminaries Herbie Hancock on piano, Bucky Pizzarelli on rhythm guitar, Grady Tate on drums, Richard Davis on bass, and Ray Barretto on percussion.

The head contains a classic Montgomery blues line made of simple single-note licks punctuated by chord jabs. His melodies throughout are drawn from the A Mixolydian (A–B–C#–D–E–F#–G) and D Mixolydian (D–E–F#–G–A–B–C) modes. In the final four measures we receive the signature Montgomery blues alterations. These are based on the sort of atypical progression for which he was famous: Bm7–C#m7 | Dmaj7–Dm7 | C#m7–Cm7 | Bm7–E7#9. Note the use of modified "West Coast changes" and pandiatonic motion (Bm7–C#m7–Dmaj7) in this cycle. Montgomery gives the phrase a strong rhythmic treatment with off-beat accents and a staccato two-note riff.

Montgomery applies his three-tier improvisation approach to the five-chorus solo. The first two choruses are in single notes, the next two are in octaves, and the fifth chorus is essentially in block chords. His single-note soloing is dominated by pentatonic and standard blues sounds with an occasional bebop reference in measures 17, 20–24, and 33–34. The playful phrase in measures 25–28 is a completely uncategorizable passage that is a unique Montgomery trait. It is comprised of slurred three-note groups repeated and moved in fifth intervals sequentially across the strings as a long glissando.

Montgomery's octave choruses also contain a mixture of blues-pentatonic and bebop playing. The most pronounced jazz phrases are in measures 45–48 and measures 53–59. The latter features a signature 16-note rhythm figure in measure 58 made of slurred octaves rising in a Bm9 (B–D–F#–A–C#) arpeggio outline. Montgomery plays this figure frequently, particularly in this three-against-four hemiola rhythm.

Montgomery's block-chord solo is a capsulized, but equally potent, version of his longer excursions of the Riverside years. Note the following trademark elements: use of his chain of diminished chords and diminished chords as substitute dominant-sevenths in measures 69–71, half-step chromatic "push chords" (G#9–A9, Eb9–D9, Bb13–A7) in measures 61–64, and chromatically descending ii–V's (Gm9–C7, F#m9–B7, Fm9–Bb7) as a modified turnaround in measures 72–73. Noteworthy also is the variety of chord colors employed for the tonic chord A: A9, A13, A6, A7, A7#5, A6/9 and even Amaj7.

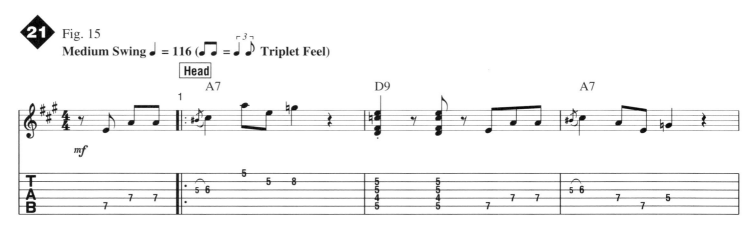

Fig. 15

Medium Swing ♩ = 116 (♩♩ = ♩♪ Triplet Feel)

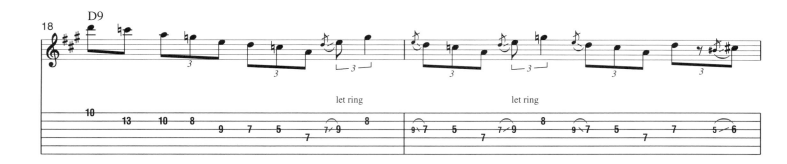

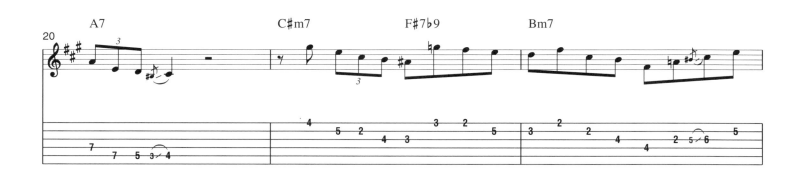

B 2nd Chorus

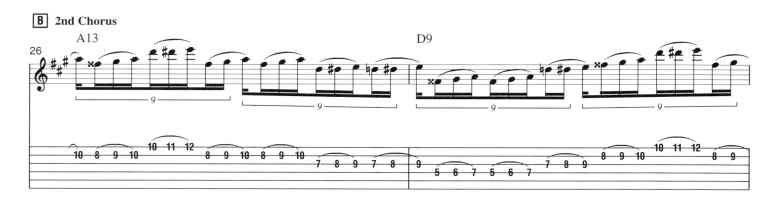

* Played ahead of the beat.

C 3rd Chorus

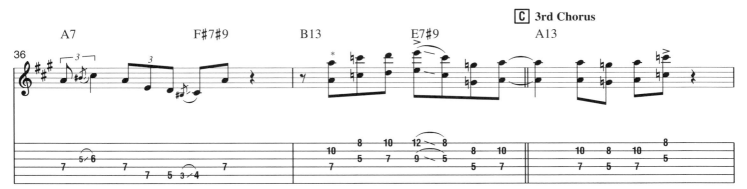

*Mute inner string of octaves throughout.

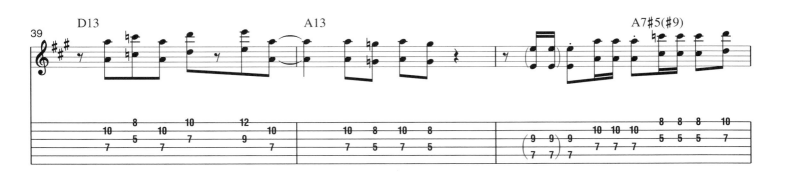

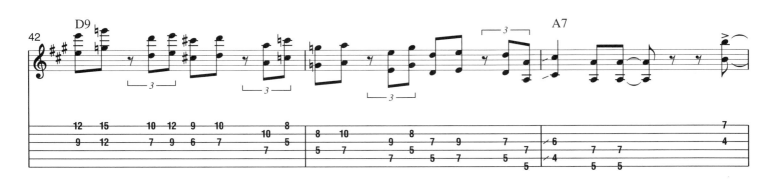

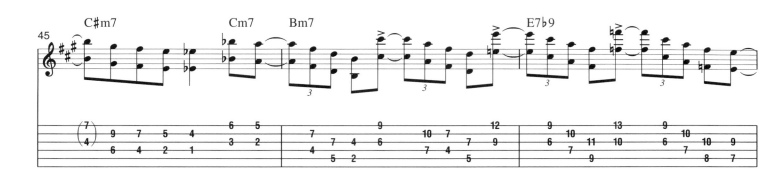

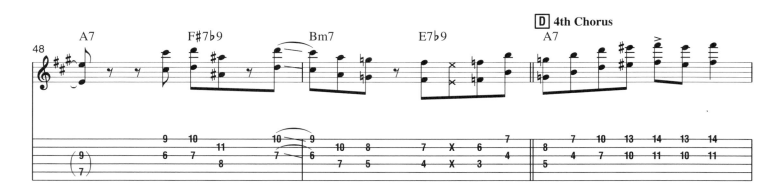

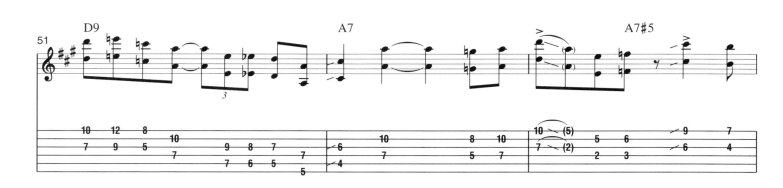

O.G.D.
(Further Adventures of Jimmy and Wes)
By John L. (Wes) Montgomery

Figure 16—Head and Solo

Wes Montgomery formed the supergroup of organ trios when he joined forces with Hammond virtuoso Jimmy Smith and drummer Grady Tate in late 1966 for the Verve albums *The Dynamic Duo* and *Further Adventures of Jimmy and Wes*. Augmenting the lineup was the ubiquitous Ray Barretto (percussion). The second record included the original Montgomery composition "O.G.D." ("The Road Song"), an abbreviation for Organ-Guitar-Drums. It is one of his most celebrated pieces. Truly a signature song, "O.G.D." is in 32-bar AABA form and features an irrepressible minor-mode line set in a medium-up Latin-funk groove. It was recorded again by Montgomery in 1968 for his last album *Road Song* on A&M Records. "The Road Song" was covered by Pat Martino on his Wes Montgomery tribute album *The Visit*, reissued as *Footprints*.

The head is played predominantly in octaves, with light chord fills in the second and fourth measures of the A sections. Its main theme is largely pentatonic, giving the tune an earthy quality befitting the title. Note the mixture of chords in the A section structure: Gm7, Am7, and Em7♭5 are derived from the G Dorian mode (G–A–B♭–C–D–E–F); Fm7, E♭maj7, and Cm7 from the E♭ major scale (E♭–F–G–A♭–B♭–C–D); and D7♭9 from the G harmonic minor scale (G–A–B♭–C–D–E♭–F♯). The bridge is distinguished by more urbane ii–V–I progressions. It modulates first to B♭ major and then to A♭ major via ii–V–I's. Note the Bm7–E7 inserted in measure 20 as a half-step approach to B♭m7. This harmonic gesture is a Montgomery harmonic trademark found in countless compositions and arrangements.

The solo is played over two choruses of the 32-bar form. Montgomery takes the first chorus in single notes and the second in octaves. Most of the lines in the A sections are derived from the modes cited above. These phrases tend to be looser and varied, and range in content from blues-inflected melodies to diatonic modal statements. Signature licks include the descending sequence in measures 35–36, the brisk, ascending linear arpeggios in measures 40–41, and the pentatonic and blues riffs in measures 56–60. The bridge finds Montgomery outlining the specific chords of the progression with bebop lines played in strings of eighth notes, adding a Baroque tone to the solo. He establishes a pattern of an arpeggio preceded by a lower neighbor note and sequences it through the changes in measures 49–54. Another highlight is the bebop line which closes the single-note solo in measures 60–64. Note the textbook outlining of the chord progression in measures 61–62, and Montgomery's decision to wrap up the chorus with a blues lick in measures 63–64.

Montgomery's octave solo also contains numerous noteworthy and memorable moments. The opening question-and-answer phrase employs a favorite rhythm pattern of staggered-eighth syncopation in measures 65 and 67. Rhythm is also an important aspect of the slurred riffs in measures 73–76. Here, Montgomery uses lower neighbor tones to emphasize E (F♭), A, and E♭ tones and sets up a recurring on-the-beat, off-the-beat pattern. Montgomery outlines many of the chord progressions of the bridge with extended arpeggios: Cm9 in measure 81, Bm11 in measure 84, and B♭m11 and E♭7 in measures 85–86. Note the signature cadential phrase in measures 86 (beat 3) and 87 (first two beats). A dramatic ascending phrase in octaves is heard in measures 89–90. The melody is almost exclusively pentatonic, with the added ninth A providing a climax to the solo. Montgomery closes on a down-home note with a paraphrase of an earlier blues melody (see measure 63) in octaves.

Head

Moderately ♩ = 154

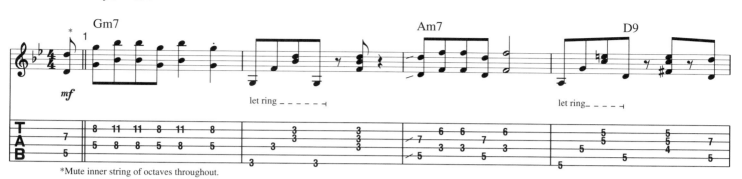

*Mute inner string of octaves throughout.

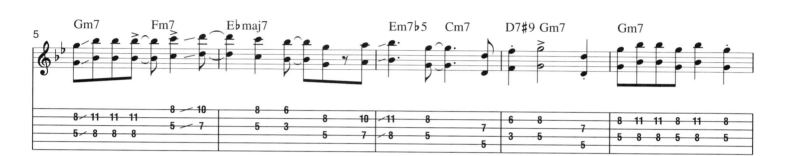

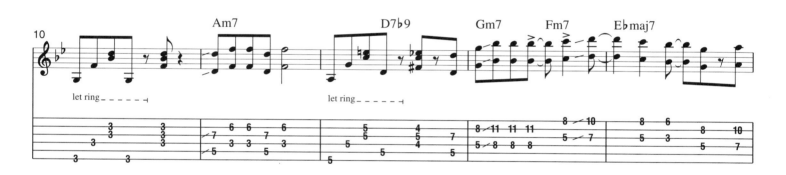

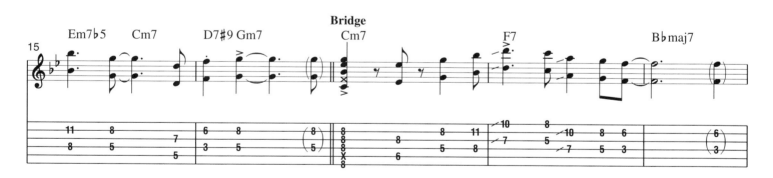

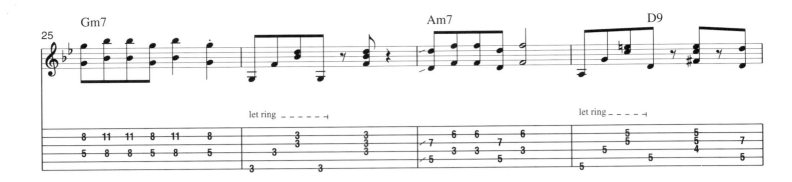

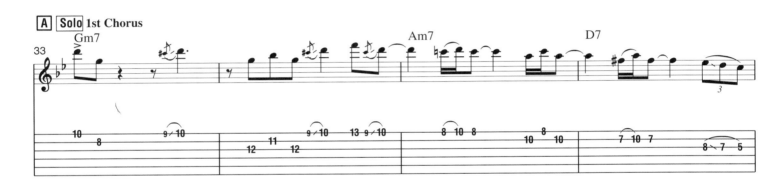

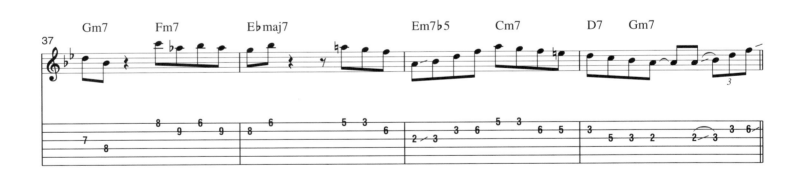

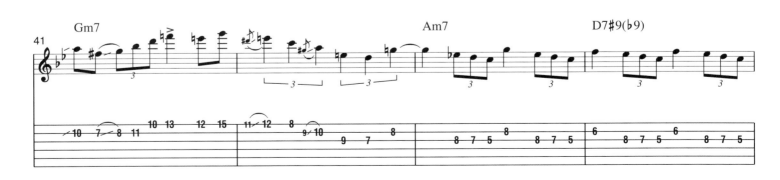

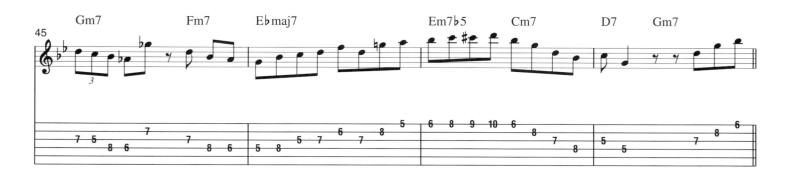

Bridge

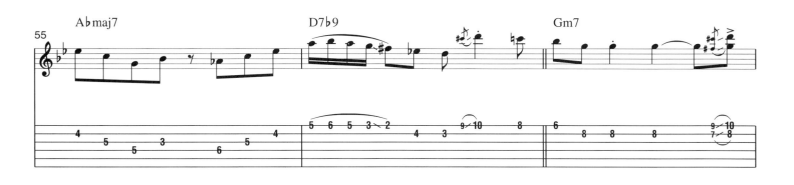

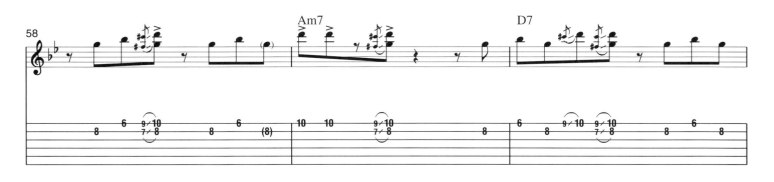

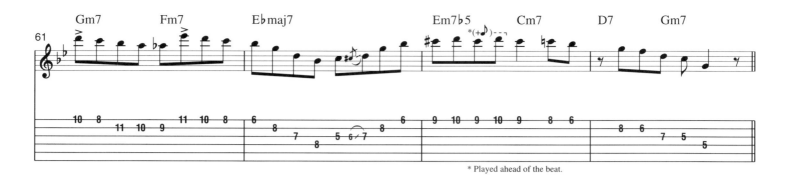

* Played ahead of the beat.

B 2nd Chorus

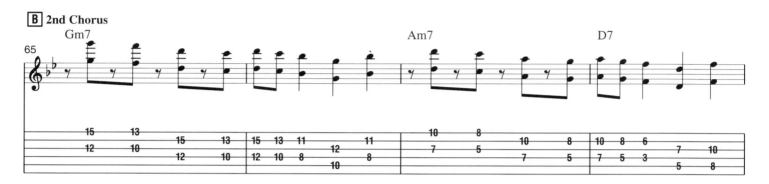

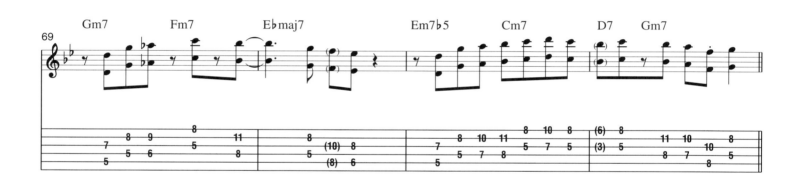

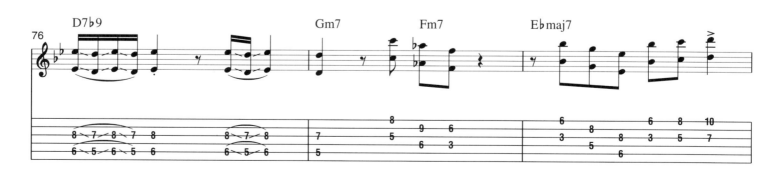

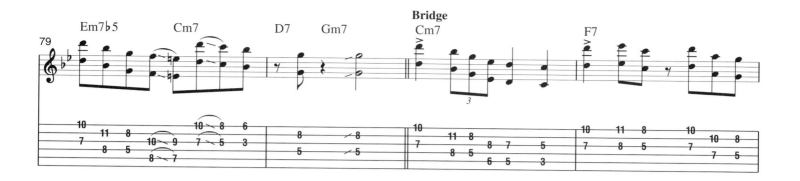

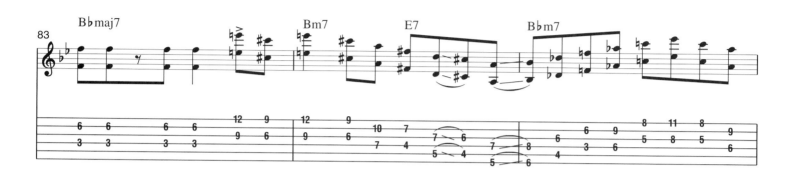

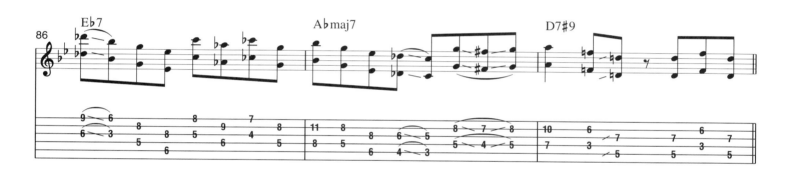

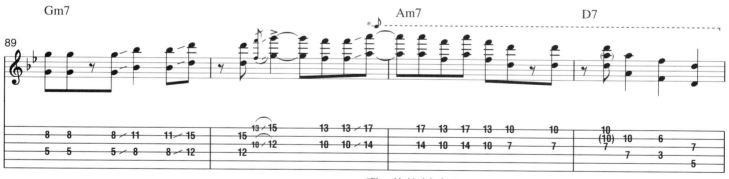

*Played behind the beat.

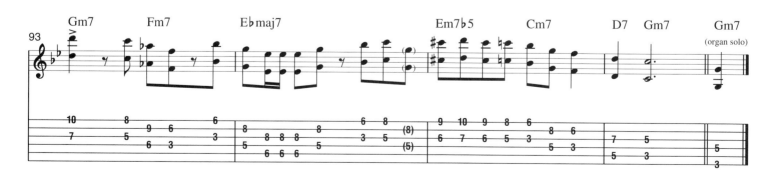

Guitar Notation Legend

Guitar Music can be notated three different ways: on a *musical staff*, in *tablature*, and in *rhythm slashes*.

RHYTHM SLASHES are written above the staff. Strum chords in the rhythm indicated. Use the chord diagrams found at the top of the first page of the transcription for the appropriate chord voicings. Round noteheads indicate single notes.

THE MUSICAL STAFF shows pitches and rhythms and is divided by bar lines into measures. Pitches are named after the first seven letters of the alphabet.

TABLATURE graphically represents the guitar fingerboard. Each horizontal line represents a a string, and each number represents a fret.

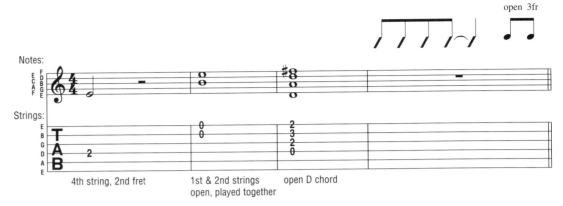

Definitions for Special Guitar Notation

HALF-STEP BEND: Strike the note and bend up 1/2 step.

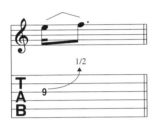

BEND AND RELEASE: Strike the note and bend up as indicated, then release back to the original note. Only the first note is struck.

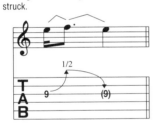

VIBRATO: The string is vibrated by rapidly bending and releasing the note with the fretting hand.

LEGATO SLIDE: Strike the first note and then slide the same fret-hand finger up or down to the second note. The second note is not struck.

WHOLE-STEP BEND: Strike the note and bend up one step.

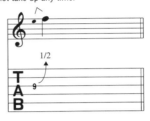

PRE-BEND: Bend the note as indicated, then strike it.

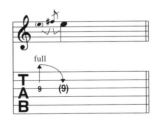

WIDE VIBRATO: The pitch is varied to a greater degree by vibrating with the fretting hand.

SHIFT SLIDE: Same as legato slide, except the second note is struck.

GRACE NOTE BEND: Strike the note and bend up as indicated. The first note does not take up any time.

PRE-BEND AND RELEASE: Bend the note as indicated. Strike it and release the bend back to the original note.

HAMMER-ON: Strike the first (lower) note with one finger, then sound the higher note (on the same string) with another finger by fretting it without picking.

TRILL: Very rapidly alternate between the notes indicated by continuously hammering on and pulling off.

SLIGHT (MICROTONE) BEND: Strike the note and bend up 1/4 step.

UNISON BEND: Strike the two notes simultaneously and bend the lower note up to the pitch of the higher.

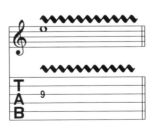

PULL-OFF: Place both fingers on the notes to be sounded. Strike the first note and without picking, pull the finger off to sound the second (lower) note.

TAPPING: Hammer ("tap") the fret indicated with the pick-hand index or middle finger and pull off to the note fretted by the fret hand.

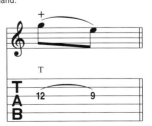

NATURAL HARMONIC: Strike the note while the fret-hand lightly touches the string directly over the fret indicated.

PINCH HARMONIC: The note is fretted normally and a harmonic is produced by adding the edge of the thumb or the tip of the index finger of the pick hand to the normal pick attack.

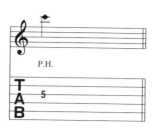

HARP HARMONIC: The note is fretted normally and a harmonic is produced by gently resting the pick hand's index finger directly above the indicated fret (in parentheses) while the pick hand's thumb or pick assists by plucking the appropriate string.

PICK SCRAPE: The edge of the pick is rubbed down (or up) the string, producing a scratchy sound.

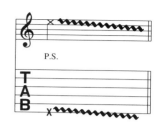

MUFFLED STRINGS: A percussive sound is produced by laying the fret hand across the string(s) without depressing, and striking them with the pick hand.

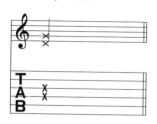

PALM MUTING: The note is partially muted by the pick hand lightly touching the string(s) just before the bridge.

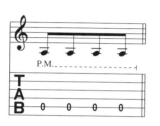

RAKE: Drag the pick across the strings indicated with a single motion.

TREMOLO PICKING: The note is picked as rapidly and continuously as possible.

ARPEGGIATE: Play the notes of the chord indicated by quickly rolling them from bottom to top.

VIBRATO BAR DIVE AND RETURN: The pitch of the note or chord is dropped a specified number of steps (in rhythm) then returned to the original pitch.

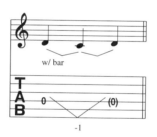

VIBRATO BAR SCOOP: Depress the bar just before striking the note, then quickly release the bar.

VIBRATO BAR DIP: Strike the note and then immediately drop a specified number of steps, then release back to the original pitch.

Additional Musical Definitions

 (accent) • Accentuate note (play it louder)

 (accent) • Accentuate note with great intensity

 (staccato) • Play the note short

 • Downstroke

 • Upstroke

D.S. al Coda • Go back to the sign (𝄋), then play until the measure marked "*To Coda*," then skip to the section labelled "*Coda*."

D.S. al Fine • Go back to the beginning of the song and play until the measure marked "*Fine*" (end).

Rhy. Fig. • Label used to recall a recurring accompaniment pattern (usually chordal).

Riff • Label used to recall composed, melodic lines (usually single notes) which recur.

Fill • Label used to identify a brief melodic figure which is to be inserted into the arrangement.

Rhy. Fill • A chordal version of a Fill.

tacet • Instrument is silent (drops out).

 • Repeat measures between signs.

 • When a repeated section has different endings, play the first ending only the first time and the second ending only the second time.

NOTE: Tablature numbers in parentheses mean:
1. The note is being sustained over a system (note in standard notation is tied), or
2. The note is sustained, but a new articulation (such as a hammer-on, pull-off, slide or vibrato begins, or
3. The note is a barely audible "ghost" note (note in standard notation is also in parentheses).

GUITAR *signature licks*

The Signature Licks book/audio packs are especially formatted to give guitarists instruction on how to play a particular artist style by using the actual transcribed, "right from the record" licks! Designed for use by anyone from beginner right up to the experienced player who is looking to expand their insight. The books contain full performance notes and an overview of each artist or group's style with transcriptions in notes and tab. The audio features full-demo playing tips and techniques, as well as playing examples at a slower tempo.

ACOUSTIC GUITAR OF '60S AND '70S
by Wolf Marshall
00695024 Book/CD Pack $19.95

ACOUSTIC GUITAR OF '80S AND '90S
by Wolf Marshall
00695033 Book/CD Pack $19.95

AEROSMITH 1973-1979
by Wolf Marshall
00695106 Book/CD Pack $19.95

AEROSMITH 1979-1998
by Wolf Marshall
00695219 Book/CD Pack $19.95

BEATLES BASS
by Wolf Marshall
00695283 Book/CD Pack $17.95

THE BEATLES FAVORITES
by Wolf Marshall
00695096 Book/CD Pack $19.95

THE BEATLES HITS
by Wolf Marshall
00695049 Book/CD Pack $19.95

THE BEST OF BLACK SABBATH
by Troy Stetina
00695249 Book/CD Pack $19.95

BLUES GUITAR CLASSICS
by Wolf Marshall
00695177 Book/CD Pack $17.95

THE BEST OF ERIC CLAPTON
by Jeff Perrin
00695038 Book/CD Pack $19.95

ERIC CLAPTON – THE BLUESMAN
by Andy Aledort
00695040 Book/CD Pack $19.95

ERIC CLAPTON – FROM THE ALBUM UNPLUGGED
by Wolf Marshall
00695250 Book/CD Pack $19.95

THE BEST OF CREAM
by Wolf Marshall
00695251 Book/CD Pack $19.95

THE BEST OF DEF LEPPARD
by Jeff Perrin
00696516 Book/CD Pack $19.95

GREATEST GUITAR SOLOS OF ALL TIME
by Wolf Marshall
00695301 Book/CD Pack $17.95

GUITAR INSTRUMENTAL HITS
by Wolf Marshall
00695309 Book/CD Pack $16.95

GUITAR RIFFS OF THE '60S
by Wolf Marshall
00695218 Book/CD pack $16.95

GUITAR RIFFS OF THE '70S
by Wolf Marshall
00695158 Book/CD Pack............$16.95

THE BEST OF GUNS N' ROSES
by Jeff Perrin
00695183 Book/CD Pack $19.95

THE BEST OF BUDDY GUY
by Dave Rubin
00695186 Book/CD Pack $19.95

JIMI HENDRIX
by Andy Aledort
00696560 Book/CD Pack $19.95

ERIC JOHNSON
by Wolf Marshall
00699317 Book/CD Pack $19.95

THE BEST OF KISS
by Jeff Perrin
00699413 Book/CD Pack $19.95

MARK KNOPFLER
by Wolf Marshall
00695178 Book/CD Pack $19.95

MEGADETH
by Jeff Perrin
00695041 Book/CD Pack $19.95

WES MONTGOMERY
00695387 Book/CD Pack $19.95

THE GUITARS OF ELVIS
by Wolf Marshall
00696507 Book/CD Pack $19.95

BEST OF QUEEN
by Wolf Marshall
00695097 Book/CD Pack $19.95

THE RED HOT CHILI PEPPERS
by Dale Turner
00695173 Book/CD Pack $19.95

THE BEST OF THE RED HOT CHILI PEPPERS FOR BASS
by Dale Turner
00695285 Book/CD Pack $17.95

THE ROLLING STONES
by Wolf Marshall
00695079 Book/CD Pack $19.95

BEST OF CARLOS SANTANA
by Wolf Marshall
00695010 Book/CD Pack $19.95

THE BEST OF JOE SATRIANI
by Dale Turner
00695216 Book/CD Pack $19.95

STEVE VAI
by Jeff Perrin
00673247 Book/CD Pack $22.95

STEVE VAI – ALIEN LOVE SECRETS: THE NAKED VAMPS
00695223 Book/CD Pack $19.95

STEVE VAI – FIRE GARDEN: THE NAKED VAMPS
00695166 Book/CD Pack $19.95

STEVIE RAY VAUGHAN
by Wolf Marshall
00699316 Book/CD Pack $19.95

THE GUITAR STYLE OF STEVIE RAY VAUGHAN
by Wolf Marshall
00695155 Book/CD Pack $19.95

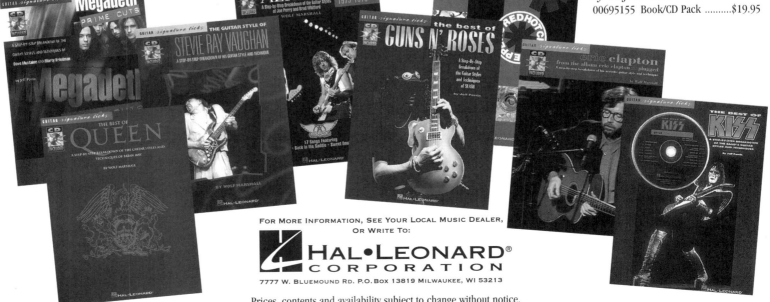

FOR MORE INFORMATION, SEE YOUR LOCAL MUSIC DEALER, OR WRITE TO:

HAL•LEONARD® CORPORATION
7777 W. BLUEMOUND RD. P.O. BOX 13819 MILWAUKEE, WI 53213

Prices, contents and availability subject to change without notice.

0200